Minding *God's* Bu$iness

Sharpening the Marketplace Prophet

ANOINTED FIRE HOUSE
CHRISTIAN PUBLISHING

Minding God's Business
Sharpening the Marketplace Prophet
by Tiffany Buckner

© 2017, Tiffany Buckner
www.tiffanybuckner.com
info@anointedfire.com

Published by Anointed Fire™ House
www.anointedfirehouse.com
Cover Design by Anointed Fire™ House

ISBN-10: 0-9993380-0-5
ISBN-13: 978-0-9993380-0-1

Minding God's Business

Sharpening the Marketplace Prophet

TIFFANY BUCKNER

Table of Contents

Introduction

Every believer has an entrepreneur locked up within him or her, and it is the job of the believer to unleash the entrepreneur within. Nevertheless, the average person has absolutely no knowledge of how to tap into the realm of marketplace ministry and for this reason, many start businesses, only to lose them in three years or less. The average business does not survive the first year, and this isn't always because of the market for whatever it is the entrepreneur is selling. In most cases, the issue is the entrepreneur.

In Minding God's Business, you will learn how to think, reason and market like the successful entrepreneur that you are. You will learn about the common spirits and maneuvers the enemy sends into the marketplace to distract, bind and rob the prophets of God. This isn't your ordinary "how to start a business" book. This is a book designed to help mold your thinking and prepare you for your journey in the realm of business.

Prophets in the Marketplace

Before we get started, let's first establish this: if you have the Holy Spirit, you are prophetic. You may not necessarily be a Prophet, but you can prophesy. You simply need to learn to tap into the prophetic realm.

Next, we need to understand that there are prophets who are specifically called to the marketplace. This doesn't mean they are not called to other areas of ministry, because they are, but God also uses them in the marketplace. He does this because the marketplace belongs to Him. The world may be dominating the financial arena right now, but this was not the way God intended it to be and this won't be the way it'll always be. This is why He said that the wealth of the wicked is laid up for the just (see Proverbs 13:22).

Throughout the Bible, God repeatedly refers to believers as vessels. In secular terms, a vessel is a large boat. There are several things that we can observe about vessels and they include, but are not limited to the following:

1. **A large boat is used to transport goods and people from one nation to the next:** Every believer has a capacity, just like every boat has a capacity. Google defines the word "capacity" this way: *the maximum amount that something can contain.* This is why God said He wouldn't put more on us than we can bear. Nevertheless, unlike natural boats, we are vessels that increase and decrease in size, both naturally and spiritually. The size of our faith will determine how much the Master trusts us with (see Matthew 25:23). The more God can trust us, the more people He will use us to lead to Him. We are basically transporting them from the kingdom of darkness to the Kingdom of God, but

only God can translate them between both kingdoms (Colossians 1:13).

2. **A trade agreement must be in place before trade operations commence:** As believers, we either ally ourselves with God or we ally ourselves with Satan through agreement. Whatever we transport is determined by who we are in agreement with. If we are worried, fearful, hateful and bitter, we have an agreement with Satan. This doesn't have to be a verbal or written agreement; we establish agreements with our hearts and those agreements will manifest themselves in our thoughts, actions and words. If we are forgiving, loving, faithful and pleasant, we have an agreement with God. This is the evidence of our faith in Him. When we agree with Him, we will tap into the joy of the Lord and the peace that surpasses all understanding. If we are a mixture of good and evil things, we are double agents (unstable people). This means that we are

vessels carrying both hot and cold water. The Bible calls this lukewarm. God also references this condition as double-mindedness, and He said in James 1:8 (KJV), "A double minded man is unstable in all his ways."

3. **Every boat has a capacity; it can store a certain number of items and hold a certain amount of weight before it starts to sink:** The same is true for people. We all have a capacity. We have varying measures of faith, knowledge, understanding, wisdom and goods. If we try to hold more than we can bear, we will sink into depression, temptation, worry, pride, etc. Now, God won't put more on us than we can bear, but we are infamous for doing this to ourselves. If we try to carry far less than we can hold, the current of life will toss us around. Understand this: a filled ship won't always need an anchor (in certain depths) because of the weight of the merchandise it's carrying.

4. **The boat's crew must always look out for stowaways on the boat:** These are people who enter the boat and hide with the intentions of illegally entering another nation. In our cases, stowaways, also known as squatters, are oftentimes demonic spirits who must be cast out of the vessels that we are. Additionally, stowaways can be those lazy friends who think they'll ride someone's anointing to the top.

5. **Most manufactured boats and ships have a certain depth that they can sail through:** A speedboat should not be found in the center of an ocean because the current there is much stronger than the current is in shallow waters. The waves could easily topple the boat and cause it to sink. Likewise, some boats can only sail in shallow water. This means that we, as believers, can venture into different measures of God's heart. Some people are deep; some people are shallow, but this does not change the fact that they

are believers. Additionally, every believer can weather a certain degree of storms. A storm that one believer easily sails through for years would be enough to topple another believer in a matter of seconds.

What we need to take from this is that, as vessels, we can only hold or endure so much. It is unwise for you, as a marketplace minister, to desire another minister's anointing. This means that you need to make peace with the measure that God has allotted you before you even enter the marketplace. There will be people who won't be as intelligent (or educated) as you and they will have better ideas, greater profits and more favor with men than you have. This is simply because God has determined that He can trust them with more. God isn't moved by our intellect; He is moved by our faith. Do not enter the marketplace comparing yourself with another human being, otherwise, you will be shipwrecked.

There are several marketplace ministers listed in the scriptures and they include:

- **Abraham:** Abraham was a cattleman (See Genesis 13:2).
- **Solomon:** Solomon was an international tradesman (Chronicles 9:13, 1 Kings 10:22-29).
- **Apostle Paul:** Apostle Paul was a tent-maker (Acts 18:3).
- **Jesus the Christ:** Jesus was a carpenter (Mark 6:3).

Additionally, Proverbs 31 talks about the noble woman who happened to be a wife and an entrepreneur.

Proverbs 31:18-24 (ESV): She perceives that her merchandise is profitable. Her lamp does not go out at night. She puts her hands to the distaff, and her hands hold the spindle. She opens her hand to the poor and reaches out her hands to the needy. She is not afraid of snow for her household, for all her household are clothed in scarlet. She makes bed coverings for herself; her clothing is fine linen and purple. Her husband is known in the gates when he sits among the elders of the land. She makes linen garments and sells them; she delivers sashes to the merchant.

God strategically positions prophets in the marketplace, just as He's placed prophets in every system utilized by man. If you are a marketplace minister, it is important that you establish boundaries (in business, relationships, financially, etc.) before you launch your business. Those boundaries will help to secure your business and keep you from falling into the snares that many of your predecessors have fallen into. Consider Lot. As we've discussed, Abram was an entrepreneur who was called by God. Once he accepted the call on his life, he did not stop being an entrepreneur. He just had to move when God said move, taking his merchandise with him. Lot was blessed simply because he walked with Abram. He didn't realize this, so familiarity crept in and his herdsmen started contending with Abram's herdsmen. This is important to know because Abram was the called one, meaning, he had a greater authority than Lot.

Genesis 12:1-4 (ESV): Now the Lord said to Abram, "Go from your country and your kindred and your father's house to the land that I will show you. And I will make of you a great nation, and I will bless you and make your name great, so that you will be a blessing. I will bless those who bless you, and him who dishonors you I will curse, and in you all the families of the Earth shall be blessed."

So, Abram went, as the Lord had told him, and Lot went with him.

Genesis 13:1-16 (ESV): So, Abram went up from Egypt, he and his wife and all that he had, and Lot with him, into the Negeb. Now Abram was very rich in livestock, in silver, and in gold. And he journeyed on from the Negeb as far as Bethel to the place where his tent had been at the beginning, between Bethel and Ai, to the place where he had made an altar at the first. And there Abram called upon the name of the Lord. And Lot, who went with Abram, also had flocks and herds and tents, so that the land could not support both dwelling together; for their possessions were so great that they could not dwell together, and there was strife between the herdsmen of Abram's livestock and the herdsmen of Lot's livestock. At that time, the Canaanites and the Perizzites were dwelling in the land.

Then Abram said to Lot, "Let there be no strife between you and me, and between your herdsmen and my herdsmen, for we are kinsmen. Is not the whole land before you? Separate yourself from me. If you take the left hand, then I will go to the right, or if you take the right hand, then I will go to the left." And Lot lifted up his eyes and saw that the Jordan Valley was well watered everywhere like the garden of the Lord, like the land of Egypt, in the direction of Zoar. (This was before the Lord destroyed Sodom and Gomorrah.) So, Lot chose for himself all the Jordan Valley, and Lot journeyed east. Thus, they separated from each other. Abram settled in the land of Canaan, while Lot settled among the cities of the valley and moved his tent as far as

Sodom. Now the men of Sodom were wicked, great sinners against the Lord.

The Lord said to Abram, after Lot had separated from him, "Lift up your eyes and look from the place where you are, northward and southward and eastward and westward, for all the land that you see I will give to you and to your offspring forever. I will make your offspring as the dust of the Earth, so that if one can count the dust of the Earth, your offspring also can be counted.

There are a few things that we can take from this text.

1. **Familiarity is an enemy of the marketplace minister:** God told Abram to leave his country and his kindred (relatives). He obeyed God by leaving, but he disobeyed God when he decided to take Lot (his nephew) with him. As a marketplace prophet, you will be tempted to take people with you who God has commanded you to leave behind. Nevertheless, if you take them with you, strife will enter and

you will eventually have to separate yourself from them.

2. **Honor is important to God:** The Lord said to Abram that He would bless those who blessed him and curse those who dishonored him. Lot dishonored Abram and this dishonor trickled down to his herdsmen. Understand this, even though the Bible does not speak of a dispute between Abram and Lot, Lot was the head (authority) over his herdsmen. If he'd honored Abram and hadn't gotten too familiar with him, his herdsmen would have been afraid to dispute with Abram's herdsmen. Therefore Abram, in all his wisdom, identified the source of the problem. He said to Lot, "Let there be no strife between you and me, and between your herdsmen and my herdsmen, for we are kinsmen." Abram identified first that the strife did not start with the herdsmen; it started with Lot. It likely hadn't manifested itself in Lot's actions, but it was in his

heart. When dishonor crept in, Abram realized that he'd made a mistake by bringing him along. Additionally, Lot was eventually taken into captivity and Abram had to go and rescue him (see Genesis 14).

3. **Our relationships are conduits that allow what's in our lives to manifest in the lives of those closest to us and vice versa:** Lot became rich just from hanging with Abram, but Abram was hindered because he hung with Lot. The text tells us that both men were so rich that the land could not hold them and all their possessions. God said that He would bless Abram and He did, but Lot, through association, tapped into that same blessing. Many believers will attempt to connect with you for this very reason. When people see the call of God on your life, especially, when you begin to bear fruit, they will go out of their way to establish close-knit relationships with you. And if you allow them to do this, they will pull

from the anointing on your life, but you will pull from the dishonor on their lives. How was Abram hindered? If you'll read the text, you'll notice that God spoke to Abram when He told him to leave his country and his kinsmen. After that, Abram did not hear from God regarding the direction He wanted him to go in. It wasn't until Abram separated himself from Lot that he heard from God again, and when God did speak, He gave Abram his next set of instructions.

4. **Ungodly or lazy people will let you pray and die to yourself, while they simply benefit from your relationship with God:** The text tells us that Abram heard and answered the call of God, Abram called upon the name of the Lord and Abram built an altar for the Lord. We don't see Lot doing any of these things. The same is true for people who, out of selfish ambition, connect with marketplace ministers. They will let you pray, watch

you die to yourself and witness the changes that God makes in you, all the while, pulling from the fruit on your life. They'll even compliment you and tell you how good those fruit are.

5. **People who illegally connect with marketplace ministers are often led by their flesh:** When Abram told Lot to separate himself from him, he told Lot to pick which direction he wanted to go in. Lot looked up and saw the beautiful Jordan Valley, near Sodom and Gomorrah. Abram was being led by the Lord, but Lot was being led by his flesh and his flesh led him into a perverted place. Pay attention and you'll notice that most of the people who leave your life will be led out of it by their flesh. Your best friend may find herself meeting a man who appears to be perfectly suited for her life. Believing that she no longer needs you, she will slowly disconnect from you to pursue that relationship. That guy was the equivalent of her Jordan

Valley. Or your best friend may be a man who met another guy who he prefers to hang out with. After mentally comparing the two of you, he suddenly realizes that he has no interest in remaining friends with you, so he stops calling and coming around. That guy was the equivalent of his Jordan Valley.

As a prophet in the marketplace, it is important for you, again, to remember that you are a vessel. As such, wherever you end up directly correlates to what you're carrying or who you're carrying. I don't think any one of us desires to leave people behind, but we cannot let the personal calls from people interrupt, contaminate or hinder God's call on our lives.

Jesus, the Entrepreneur

Jesus was and is a vessel. He not only carried the Word of God, but He was the Word manifested in the flesh (see John 1:1). He carried our redemption and He traveled from region to region, proclaiming the gospel and setting the captives free.

Jesus never ceased to exist. Sure, we know that He was crucified and died on the cross (see John 19); He went and took back the keys to Hades (see Acts 2:31, Ephesians 4:8-9), He was resurrected and walked the Earth for 40 days before His ascension (see Acts 1:3), and He is now in Heaven seated on the right hand of God (see Mark 16:19). Again, Jesus never ceased to exist, just as we will never cease to exist. This is because we are spirit beings, and even though our bodies will pass away, our spirits do not and cannot pass away. Our spirits are eternal and therefore we will either spend eternity in Heaven or eternity in the lake of fire. Jesus never stopped being about the Father's business, even when He went to Hades.

Jesus was a carpenter; we all know this, but what exactly do carpenters do? Studentscholarships.org gives us a clear description of a carpenter's job and it reads: *"Carpenters construct, erect, install, and repair structures and fixtures made from wood and other materials"* *(www.studentscholarship.org/ Scholarships).*

Wood is often used to represent humanity when, of course, it is connected to a living tree. Acacia wood is often used to represent Jesus Christ because of its durability. Jesus said in John 15:5 (ESV), "I am the vine; you are the branches. Whoever abides in me and I in him, he it is that bears much fruit, for apart from me you can do nothing."

Another reference to wood is in Genesis 6, when the Lord gave Noah instructions to build an ark. The ark itself is a picture of salvation through Jesus Christ. Needless to say, the wooden ark represents Jesus. So, it is fitting that Jesus' natural occupation was carpentry.

Mark 6:3 (ESV): "Is not this the carpenter, the son of Mary and brother of James and Joses and Judas and Simon? And are not his sisters here with us?" And they took offense at him.

In this text, we come to understand Jesus' profession. In the Biblical days, the son would inherit the business of his father. Joseph, the man who raised Jesus as his own son, was a carpenter and, for this reason, Jesus became a carpenter. Traditionally, we know that carpenters build things from wood. Nevertheless, many theologians reason that because of the region Jesus was in, the word "carpenter" was more of a reference to Him being a stonemason. Nevertheless, one thing we know for sure: Jesus was an entrepreneur. This means that the entrepreneur who lives within us is Jesus Christ Himself.

Romans 8:10 (ESV): But if Christ is in you,

although the body is dead because of sin, the Spirit is life because of righteousness.

Like Jesus, we aren't just marketplace ministers; we are called to destroy the works of Satan. We destroy his works in the marketplace by learning to dominate that sphere. This means that, like Jesus, we will experience quite a bit of opposition. This opposition is demonic, but it has no power over us unless we submit to it. We are miniature arks, carrying the Word of God to unbelievers and helping to carry one another in times of hardship.

What I find interesting about the Lord is that even though He was a carpenter, He didn't market His skills or Himself in the church; He promoted God and God only. This is an important lesson for us if we intend to pattern ourselves after Him. Consider Abram (later renamed Abraham). He followed the voice of the Lord and took his merchandise (cattle, livestock, earthly goods) with him. This means that his business was led by his ministry and not the other way around.

Not much is known about Jesus' life as an entrepreneur, but what we do know is that He was able to turn the hearts of many back to God. This is an amazing feat, considering the Jews were devoutly religious people who would kill to preserve their beliefs. Nevertheless, Jesus knew how to successfully promote God. Below are a few things we can take from Jesus' life:

1. **God must be first:** Jesus promoted, God, the Father. After His ministry began, we don't hear anything else about Him being a carpenter. This doesn't mean that we ought to close our businesses and pursue ministry full-time. What we should take from this is God must be the head of everything we do if we want what we do to prosper.

2. **Never market self:** Jesus is the Christ, but this wasn't something He went around shouting. As a matter of fact, He asked Peter, "Who do man say that I

am?" After that, He asked him, "Who do you say that I am?"

3. **Faith over money:** The world promotes this ideology that money should be over everything. We've heard this in the music, saw it demonstrated in the movies, etc. However, we have never read a story about Jesus pursuing money. He used money because it was a part of the system He was in, but He did not allow the love of money to bind Him. As a marketplace minister, one thing you'll come to understand is anytime you pursue money, it will run away from you, but when you pursue the heart of God, money will be attracted to you.

4. **Humility is key:** Jesus had many opportunities to show Himself powerful for the sake of promoting Himself. However, He did not perform miracles to entertain people; He was genuinely concerned about the people of God, so He performed miracles to loose them from the bondage that sin

had enslaved them to. Matthew 12:38-39 (ESV) reads, "Then some of the scribes and Pharisees answered him, saying, 'Teacher, we wish to see a sign from you.' But he answered them, 'An evil and adulterous generation seeks for a sign, but no sign will be given to it except the sign of the prophet Jonah.'" Jesus could have shown them a sign and silenced them, but He wanted to save them, not entertain them.

5. **Never compromise the faith:** Jesus was given many opportunities to compromise, but He recognized them for what they were: opportunities from the enemy. As a matter of fact, the Bible tells us that Jesus was led into the wilderness to be tempted by Satan. As marketplace ministers, you will be tempted, but regardless of how great the temptation is, you are able to bear it or, better yet, resist it. If you compromise the faith for the sake of prospering yourself, you have allowed the enemy to buy you out. You've

switched teams. Believe it or not, many believers have willfully compromised their faith and started prostituting their heavenly gifts. Their compromises may have been profitable financially, but morally and spiritually, those believers are bankrupt.

6. **Show some fruit:** What is the evidence of your faith? Where is the evidence that you are trusting God in regards to your business? Understand this: just as our lives are supposed to give glory to God, our businesses should give God glory. Jesus cast out demons, raised the dead, healed the sick, turned water into wine, and fed five thousand people with five loaves of bread and two fish. He did this to promote the Kingdom of God. In business, we must remind ourselves that what we do is for the glory of God and not for our own selfish benefit. When God is first in our businesses, He will produce much fruit through us,

and the evidence of our faith will draw souls to Him. Remember, we are miniature arks and as such, we should be carrying the fruit of our faith. This is the evidence that we are godly vessels.

Jesus did and said many things that we can apply to our entrepreneurial journeys, but we must remember that in all things, He kept God first and we must do the same. We are vessels of God.

The Entrepreneurial Realm

Every mindset is a realm; it is a realm of thinking, a realm of understanding, and a realm of reasoning. But before we can go further, we must examine the word "realm." Google defines the word "realm" as:

1. A royal domain; kingdom.
2. The region, sphere, or domain within which anything occurs, prevails, or dominates.

Sure, these definitions of "realm" use geographical terms, but the reality is, every person is a kingdom within himself or herself.

In our personal kingdoms, there is a king who sits on the throne of our hearts. This king is the governing authority over our lives. He has been elected by us, and therefore, He lives within us in accordance with our wills. For some people, the king of their lives is

Satan. For some, their bellies (appetites and lusts) are their kings (see Philippians 3:19), and of course, for some, the King of kings (Jesus Christ) is seated on the thrones of their hearts. Whomever your king is, you will serve, not just with lip service, but in conversation and in deed.

Matthew 15:8-9 (ESV): This people honors me with their lips, but their heart is far from me; in vain do they worship me, teaching as doctrines the commandments of men.

In the aforementioned scripture, the Lord is referencing double-minded believers. These are the believers who acknowledge Him as their Lord and Savior, but their hearts are not in His Kingdom. This means that they are citizens of sin, even though they claim to be citizens of righteousness.

The word "heart," in the biblical text references the mind or, better yet, soul of a man. The soul is comprised of the mind, will and emotions. Therefore, the Lord is saying that a believer who worships Him with their mouths, even though their hearts are far from Him, are believers who do not have Him as King over their lives. They are not serving Him, and therefore, they are not in Him. Therefore, He said that they worship Him in vain.

The entrepreneurial realm can be accessed by believers and unbelievers alike. This is because we are seed-bearing creatures who God has pre-deposited the seeds of success into. This is also because we have the mind of Christ who, Himself, is an entrepreneur. **Romans 11:28-29 (ESV):** As regards the gospel, they are enemies for your sake. But as regards election, they are beloved for the sake of their forefathers. For the gifts and the calling of God are irrevocable.

The word "irrevocable" means irreversible. Other biblical translations use the term "without repentance," meaning that regardless of a person's spiritual condition, that person has access to the gifts that God has deposited within himself or herself.

Needless to say, when unbelievers access the entrepreneurial realm, they do so illegally. How is this? Matthew 6:33 establishes the order that God wants us to follow. It reads, "But seek first the Kingdom of God and his righteousness, and all these things will be added to you" (ESV). Anytime we do not follow this order, we are operating in perversion and therefore, our deeds, seeds and harvests are illegal. Therefore, God said, in Proverbs 13:22 (ESV), "A good man leaves an inheritance to his children's children, but the sinner's wealth is laid up for the righteous."

The wealth of the wicked isn't just a wicked man's material possessions; a man's wealth is his knowledge, his inheritance, his finances and every good thing that God has pre-ordained for the believer to have. For example, we see an overabundance of children being born to single mothers. In the biblical days, a man's children were representations of his wealth. Therefore, a fatherless child was not just a child without an inheritance in the natural realm; a fatherless child is an opportunity for a man to create a good name for himself. How so? The Bible says that God told Abraham He'd make him a father of many nations. He wasn't just referencing Abraham's children; He was referencing anyone who was grafted into righteousness because of Abraham's faith. **Galatians 3:7 (ESV):** Know then that it is those of faith who are the sons of Abraham.

Of course, faith is a realm; it is the ability to access the blessings of God by embracing the heart of God. It is submission through belief. We believe God and therefore, we submit to Him. Many people acknowledge Him with their mouths, but they do not believe Him, which means, they do not have faith. Their service to Him is centered around fear, lack of knowledge, hope, and familial culture. For example, a child can be brought up by religious parents who scare the child into submitting to God, instead of teaching that child how to have a personal relationship with the Lord. That child will likely grow up saying what he heard his parents and church saying, even though he doesn't necessarily believe it. This means that he does not have faith because faith, outside of a relationship, is non-existent.

The entrepreneurial realm is where we go (mentally) to access ideas and strategies. Understand this: we are solutions, and therefore, we have within us the ability to solve the many problems that plague the earth today. Adam was a solution; Eve was a solution. Genesis 2:5 (ESV) tells us why Adam was created. It reads, "When no bush of the field was yet in the land and no small plant of the field had yet sprung up—for the Lord God had not caused it to rain on the land, and there was no man to work the ground, and a mist was going up from the land and was watering the whole face of the ground— then the Lord God formed the man of dust from the ground and breathed into his nostrils the breath of life, and the man became a living creature."

Genesis 2:18 (ESV) tells us why Eve was created. It reads, "Then the Lord God said, "It is not good that the man should be alone; I will make him a helper fit for him." As we can see, Eve was the solution to Adam's loneliness (not in state of mind, but in reality). She was the solution to a problem that God saw. We are all solutions to problems, and therefore, we possess the solutions to problems, after all, mankind is a seed-bearing creation who reproduces after himself.

Just like any territory, there is a route one must take to access the entrepreneurial mind. We cannot simply venture off blindly into this territory; it must be intentionally sought after. This doesn't mean that God doesn't give us random ideas, because He does. What it means is that we must do something about the ideas that He gives us. For example, God could give a man the idea for a new type of car, but in its seed stage, it's just an idea. It is up to the man to birth that idea into the natural realm. This means that he can't just get up and birth a car; he must learn and master the process of pushing out his idea. If he is immature and does not follow the right procedure, he may do like millions of Americans have done and that is, he will tell people about his idea before he protects that idea with a copyright, trademark or patent. Consequentially, someone will steal his idea and follow the proper steps to bringing it to life.

Additionally, every seed has stages. You can plant an apple tree, but there are stages that the tree must go through before it starts to produce fruit. Likewise, a child, after conception, must go through the gestation period before that child can be born healthy. The same is true for the ideas that God gives us. We cannot just run off and start developing them without going through whatever process that God has assigned us to go through. Every man's process is unique to himself and it is dependent upon his relationship with God, his relationship with money and his relationship with people. Each one of these realms must be governed by God before the man can give birth to a healthy, godly business. If he has a wrongful relationship with money, for example, it is easy for him to venture off into idolatry. In the realm of idolatry, he will find himself serving Mammon, the principality behind the love of money. If the man seeks and puts God first, his relationship with people and money will fall into their proper places.

I was a babe in Christ when I started desiring to work for myself. One of the first businesses I attempted to establish was a virtual interior design business. I had no experience in interior design, other than my own home, but my experiences in decorating the house that I lived in was something I enjoyed and something I received a lot of compliments on. For this reason, I decided that I wanted to be an Interior Designer. I didn't realize that I am just creative, which translated to me being passionate about the realm of design altogether. I was tapping into the creativity that was in me, but I wasn't mature enough to give birth to it. For this reason, I heard about a program that people with no design skills could use to build websites and I built my own website using that program. That website looked awful, but I was proud of it. It goes without saying that I didn't make a single sale because my website looked pitiful, the pictures I'd taken of my home were grainy and I had no system in place.

Less than a year later, I heard the Lord say that I was going to become a Web Designer. I wasn't thinking about starting a business at that particular moment, however. Not long after hearing the Lord speak those words, I built a hip hop website, featuring up and coming hip hop artists. I tried to keep things clean, telling the artists that I would not feature profane music on my site, nevertheless, the lyrics were oftentimes raunchy. This was the evidence that I was still immature and it wasn't yet the season for me to give birth to my web design business. A year or two later, the Lord told me to shut down that business and I repented for even starting it. I committed my hands to God and decided to work for the Kingdom of God only. This was the evidence that I was beginning to mature, but it does not mean that I was ready to start my business yet.

I was ridiculed by a few people for shutting down my hip hop site because it had started getting quite a bit of attention. Nevertheless, I was determined to please the Lord, even though I was still immature in the faith. I waited until God released me (a year or two later) to start my web design business and when I did, like everything else we do, I entered that realm as a rookie. I had to grow into my new gifting, which meant making a lot of mistakes that most seasoned Designers would not make. One of those mistakes was partnering up with a friend of mine, simply because I was tired of being taken advantage of by some of the customers I had. I hated being what I considered "mean" and I felt like she had the personality I needed to deal with dominant, persistent customers. I didn't realize that I simply needed to put some rules in place, have my customers sign contractual agreements and raise my prices. For this reason, I brought my friend in as a business partner, sharing half of the business I had at that time with her. She had no design skills whatsoever, so I committed to training her. Nevertheless, she was impatient and overly determined to start making money immediately. Additionally, she wanted to jump straight into delegating. By this time, I'd become a pretty decent Designer and I'd learned a lot about the business side of design, but she knew nothing about this realm. Before partnering with her, I would randomly work on my site and any other ideas that I had, but the day after our partnership was established, she told me that as business partners, I was supposed to get her clearance before I did anything on the site. This meant that those sudden ideas from Heaven would have to be cleared by her before they could be put into place. Of course, I didn't agree to this, so she stopped working for the business before she'd even started.

Now, she wasn't the problem; I was. God had given me a business, but because of my immaturity, I tried to avoid going too far outside my comfort zone by simply handing some of my responsibilities to someone else. I had to close that business because I found myself working tirelessly day in and day out with no help from her. One day, I realized that I could possibly build a multi-million dollar empire and I'd have to share it with her if I didn't close that company while it was still in its infancy. At that time, I was making maybe $150 a month, not because the market for web design was bad, but because I didn't have the keys to the right places in the entrepreneurial realm.

When a person is immature, that person will try to bring people with him or her into the entrepreneurial realm — people who God has not cleared to enter those realms. Many businesses close because of familiarity. Additionally, many businesses close because the business owners come face to face with an area of their personalities that is desperately in need of transformation. Instead of getting the deliverance, wisdom, and healing they need, they turn to other people when God wanted them to turn to Him. Understand this: in seeking God, we will begin to find areas of our souls that have been conformed to the world. We will also find areas of our souls where we need deliverance. To seek the Kingdom of God first doesn't mean you must be super spiritual before God grants you legal access to the entrepreneurial realm; it means that God is first and foremost in your life. It means that your motives are pure and money isn't your greatest motivation. In other words, when you find an area that needs transformation or deliverance, if God is first in your life, you will seek to expand the Kingdom of God within you by taking back those areas and submitting them to God. This means you may have to stop building on the business for one or more seasons so that you can let God tear down the demonic altars that have been erected in your heart and let Him heal you wherever you are wounded. If you do not do this, the darkness in you will begin to contaminate your business. Therefore, so many Christians have sin-seasoned businesses, books and music.

The entrepreneurial realm is where you'll go to access ideas, strategies and everything you'll need to build a successful business. However, this realm is not a realm of your personality; it is a region of the Kingdom of God and therefore, you must align it with the heart of God. It's very similar to the United States government. The federal government is higher than the state government, and the state government is higher than the municipal (city) government. This means that the city government is subject to the state and the state is subject to the federal. When you are a believer accessing the realm of entrepreneurship, you must govern your business with the fear of God; that way, the Lord is King of kings in your business and life. This means that He has His proper place and you won't compromise with the enemy to turn a buck.

Your Lane

Have you ever heard someone say, "Folks need to just stay in their lanes!" If you haven't heard this, as a business owner, you will hear it a lot from jealous souls or people who lack understanding. What they mean, in most cases, is if you are running an app-building business, you shouldn't venture off into, for example, selling cupcakes. Well, someone should have told this to Google, Amazon or Apple because these companies have not allowed people or labels to designate them to one or two lanes. Instead, they saw different markets, re-branded themselves and invested in those markets time and time again.

Some of the people who will tell you to stay in your lane are well-meaning, and it is true that you should not try to invest into too many ideas at once. It is a good idea to master one business before launching another one. However, there will be times when God gives you ideas that He will urge you to begin pushing out. Oftentimes, these ideas may be directly related to the business you have or they may be businesses that God wants to use to generate income for your main business. For example, I create seals and logos. However, in the past, there were seasons when the sales would slow down drastically. One day, the Lord impressed upon my heart to launch my publishing company. I didn't launch the company because I needed money; I launched it because God laid it on my heart to do so, plus, I had a lot of free time on my hands. I realized that I could either spend that time or invest it. I could spend it, for example, watching television, playing games or talking on the phone, or I could invest it into the ideas that God had given me. I launched the company and I immediately noticed that during the seasons where seal and logo sales would slow down, my publishing company's sales would accelerate. God was simply finding another way to give seed to the sower. He was also expanding my knowledge as it relates to entrepreneurship because, at that time, my knowledge was limited to graphic design only. Thankfully, I ignored the religious rantings of people who simply did not understand my assignment because, quite frankly, it was not their assignment.

Your lane is not only the gifting that God has availed to you, but it's the uniqueness of your gift that helps you to not fall into the snares of competition. Whenever you compete with another business, you must repeatedly watch that business, meaning, you won't hear from Heaven regarding what God wants you to do because you'll be too busy monitoring what someone else is doing. This would only open you up for the spirit of fear to creep in. This simply means you have a kingdom that you should be minding, but you keep visiting someone else's domain to see what that person is doing. Many companies fall into this snare and never recover because their competitors will eventually create something that intimates them and this will cause them to become discouraged. When you simply focus on the unique and complex ideas that God gives you, you will become an innovator in whatever field you are working in. For example, because I had no former training in seal and logo design, I was not limited to the rules of that market. Consequentially, I would receive customers' orders where the customers wanted entirely too much text on their designs. This was a problem, so I had to create a solution. God gave me an idea to start creating 3D style boxes at the bottom of those designs to accommodate the excessive text. He also gave me an idea to use one of the round shapes in my design program to accommodate the extra text. I'd looked at many seals and logos to see how they were supposed to be created and I'd never seen this done, but I decided to do it anyway. Those ideas became unique fingerprints of my company and before long, my customer base started increasing. Additionally, I started receiving messages from people on social media who were familiar with some of my unique fingerprints in business. Anytime they saw someone using a design of mine illegally or someone who had a design that looked like one of my designs, they would reach out to me. I soon discovered that my ideas had taken off and many new and old designers were implementing them into their designs. This is called being an innovator; this is when you've created your mark on a particular realm.

You can access the entrepreneurial realm prematurely, and when this happens, you will chase titles, recognition and money. For example, I started ministering to a woman a few years ago. She was bound to a lot of demonic realms, including fornication. A few people had attempted to minister to her, but to no avail, so when I started ministering to her, I knew that I was dealing with a stronghold. I didn't understand much about strongholds back then, but I knew a simple conversation would not be enough to get her to turn away from her sins. The woman loved God and wanted to serve Him, but she just didn't know how. I began ministering to her and I started seeing a little progress, but not a lot. After she backslid a few times, I started leading her to windows that I shouldn't have led her to. I started telling her about the benefits of serving God. I told her about the many books God had given me to write; I showed her the businesses that God had given me to run and I appealed to her desire to be in a committed relationship by telling her about the many places my ex (who was my husband at the time) had taken me. This worked. She saw all of what she'd been chasing in sin and she decided to commit to a life of abstinence in an attempt to get these things from God. This was error on my part because she didn't chase the heart of God; instead, she chased the hand of God, hoping that by serving Him, she'd get the desires of her unchanged heart. She remained abstinent for five months and this surprised her, however, because her abstinence was not centered around love, it did not work. Eventually, she returned to everything she'd once physically turned away from because she hadn't spiritually turned away from those things. In other words, she had not yet embraced repentance. This meant that her access to the entrepreneurial realm was premature. She started finding many seeds (ideas not ready to be birthed) and she tried to push them out, but to no avail. The Lord eventually dealt with me because in my attempt to lead her away from fornication, I led her straight into another realm of idolatry. Of course, I repented and learned a valuable lesson from it.

You must invest your love, heart and time into getting closer to God before you can legally access the realm of the entrepreneur. Again, you can illegally or prematurely access it at any time, but if you want to be led to the realm of true success, you must follow God's established order and that is, you must seek the Kingdom of God and all His righteousness first. Once you do this, God will add everything else (ideas, strategies, witty inventions) to you.

Systems of Success

Every kingdom has a system. A system is a way that things are done. For example, if you pay attention to the things you do every day, you will come to understand what your system is. Maybe you wake up at a certain time, take a shower, grab a cup of coffee, read your Bible and then start getting ready for work. At work, you greet everybody, find your way to your station, take a break at a certain time, complain to certain people, and then go home. Back at home, you go straight to the kitchen to cook dinner for yourself and your family. After that, you watch a little television, browse the Internet for an hour or so, go take a bath, and then head to bed. This is the system you've created for yourself. Now, you can venture outside of this system without breaking it. For example, you may wake up later on your off days, and instead of taking a shower immediately upon waking up, you may make breakfast for yourself instead. Additionally, you can deviate from your system on days when you normally follow your system; for example, you can forgo the cup of coffee in the morning, refuse to greet your co-workers because you're not in the mood for it, and go straight to bed when you come home. This won't break your system of doing things; it's just you taking a miniature vacation from it.

I teach writer's classes and one of the things I teach the students is that writing a book involves offending, challenging and even breaking their systems. During their first week in class, I warn them that they'll likely be excited in the first week of writing because our systems will allow us to take short vacations from them with no interruptions. However, once our systems are threatened, we will start to witness how strong our systems are. I have the students to commit to writing a certain number of pages each day and a certain number of pages each week. Because they must write so much, they must interrupt their systems. They are excited and proactive the first week of class, but during the second and third week, they begin to feel the strength of their systems. Some people quit the class, while others start making excuses. However, one of the strategies that God gave me was to charge each student for late homework submissions. So, for example, if the student was supposed to write twenty pages that particular week, that student could not submit the book to me until he or she had written 20 pages. If the student's book went past the deadline I set, the student had to pay a twenty dollar fee. What God was doing was taking from a system that was stronger than the systems that were keeping them from writing and using it to challenge their daily routines. As a result, the percentage of students who completed the program and their first books increased from 60 percent to 90 percent. The reason is, if a person can find a way to do what God wants them to do without breaking a system that's binding them, they will stay bound. To break one system, you must utilize another system.

The system of success can and often does involve repetitious behavior but, at the same time, the person who has entered the realm of success is not bound by those repetitions. Again, I have a seal and logo business; I can create a beautiful seal in fifteen minutes, but there are times when I don't have seal orders. There are times when I'm unable to utilize systems that I have familiarized myself with because the customer wants something completely outside of what I'm accustomed to creating. However, I cannot turn the customer away just because he or she is taking me outside my comfort zone. Instead, those type of orders are lessons designed to help expand your business by expanding your knowledge. For example, I used to see round logos with the text following the path of the logo. I didn't know how to do this and I wasn't actively trying to learn. One day, I received an order for a seal and a logo from a customer. The man was extremely manipulative, plus, he wanted a round logo with the text following the path of the logo. I allowed that man to lead me outside of the system God had given me because he kept saying he was going to give me a nice tip once I was done. Normally, with the package he had, I would revise the logo one time and if the customer wanted another revision, they'd have to pay me for it. Nevertheless, because I was still maturing in my business, I held to his promise and not God's promise. I ended up revising that logo maybe 20 times and he was not going to stop having me revise it. I had to finally tell him that I'd revise it one more time, but after that, I would have to charge him revision fees. He agreed and after I revised the logo, he paid his balance, told me how great my service was and went away. I never saw that tip he promised me. I did, however, learn how to follow a round path. I forgave the guy, of course, but I never forgot that order because I learned two valuable lessons through it, and both of those lessons have helped me to garner the measure of success I have today. First, I learned to stay within my own rules regardless of how nice a person is. I learned to never trust a flattering tongue because it's being charged by deception. Next, I learned to follow a round path. Fifty percent of my customers order round logos. So, he wasn't a waste of my time; he was someone God used to teach me two invaluable lessons.

A business with no system in place is a hobby. If a company is to be successful, the business owner must establish rules that he or she is not willing to violate, even for their nicest customers or biggest tippers. Additionally, the owner must establish a set pricing schedule, professional branding, a list of frequently asked questions, business hours and a budget. What I've learned is that anytime I allow my emotions to lead me outside of my system, I end up spending more time and more resources on that particular customer. I had to learn to firmly stand by my rules, prices and allowances to succeed. Understand this: your customers could care less about your system or your bills. There are many people out there who will try to lure you outside of the way you do business because they don't like rules; they do not like structure. They want you to follow their systems. You will mainly attract these types of customers when your business is new and you're still in that insecure stage. Nevertheless, if you do not follow the instructions in this book and you go outside your system, one of two things will happen. Either you will become frustrated with being an entrepreneur and close your business altogether or you'll get tired of being taken advantage of and start enforcing the rules you have set in place.

In addition to creating systems, you must be flexible enough to break the ones that are not working or abandon the ones that are no longer generating the type of results you want. You can outgrow a system. For example, you can make jewelry from home as long as you're not receiving a lot of orders, but once your orders increase, you must create a new system to manage the orders. You may have to hire people or work more hours. Additionally, a system can become outdated. For example, if the wholesaler goes up on the prices you normally pay for your supplies (including shipping), you will have to update your system. Therefore, it is professional suicide to charge too low for your products and services.

Lastly, systems do expire, and when they do, you need to establish and enforce new systems. For example, when I started my business, I didn't charge my customers an upfront fee. Additionally, I didn't have rules, detailing how many revisions a customer could receive with one order. Because of this, I would get requests from hopefuls — these are people who have no money or do not agree with the posted pricing, nevertheless, they want to see what you can do. They reason within their hearts that if you do everything they want you to do, they will consider paying you. Of course, they won't tell you this. They just submit their order requests and wait for you to produce what they want. Once you submit something to them, they will either complain about what you've produced or keep requesting endless revisions. Once they are satisfied with whatever it is that you've done or you refuse to revise the work, they will attempt to get a discount or, in most cases, they'll abandon the project. This type of customer is a time consumer and the only way around him or her is to have a solid system in place. Additionally, you cannot allow a customer's flattery, rigid tone or threats to persuade you to come out of your system. I've gotten customers who started their orders off using harsh tones and threatening verbiage, however, I take authority by professionally and kindly telling them the rules, pricing and by refusing to come outside of those rules. In some cases, I have to use an authoritative, but professional, tone to get them to understand that I will not be bullied. It is their personal systems to antagonize people, especially when their money is involved. If you allow them to bully you, they will temporarily or permanently disable your business.

The system of success is a system created

with no fear of failure. No business fails; only business owners fail to make the necessary adjustments to their businesses, pay the required fees or follow the established rules. Businesses never fail, but the people who run them do. What this means is if I started a t-shirt business that wasn't turning a profit, the normal response would be to close that business. This is like abandoning a car on the side of the road just because the tires have gone flat. However, a success-driven person will look for reasons why the business isn't succeeding. Some of the things to check would be:

1. **Prices:** Are the prices too low or too high? It is good to check the competitor's rates to get a better understanding of the industry standard rates for the services or products you provide.
2. **Location:** If there is a physical location, it may be in a bad area. The owner should consider relocating.
3. **Employee morale:** Employee morale, when low, will bleed over and manifest

as bad customer service. For example, there is a restaurant not too far from my house that I once liked to frequent. The restaurant sells some pretty good food, however, the woman who takes the orders (90% of the time) has a really bad attitude. For this reason, I stopped eating at that restaurant because no one wants to eat food prepared or handed over by someone who makes them feel like they've violated one of the seven deadly sins by placing an order.

4. **Branding:** Bad branding is poisonous to a business because it sends a message to the customer. The customer then sees the company as a low-budget, small business being run by someone who is trying to make a few bucks here and there. This causes customers to revert to what I call the "bootleg" or "alley" mindset. In other words, they start treating you like you're selling bootleg CDs in an ally. For this reason, some customers will

try to bargain or barter with you.

5. **Lack of Branding:** A company without a website is a company that is restricted in its sales because its reach is limited to people who live locally.

6. **Lack of Advertising:** Honestly, if I'm overwhelmed with work, I won't advertise my services until I get caught up. There was a period, however, when I wouldn't get any customers unless I promoted what I was doing. I got deleted a lot on Facebook during that season, but I also reached a lot of customers.

7. **Target Market:** Every business has a target market, which consists of people who are more likely to purchase whatever it is that they're selling. Target markets are determined by age, race, gender, socioeconomic status, and so on. For example, if I decided to make and sell broaches, I would market my products to women who are 50 years and older, ordinarily professional women and women in the

church. I would not rent an office near a college campus and attempt to sell broaches there. One of the number one destroyers of small businesses is lack of knowledge. This includes a business owner not knowing his or her target audience, which translates in that business owner attempting to market his or her business to the wrong people.

8. **Lack of Budget:** You need to know how much your company is bringing in and how much of the net income you are going to put back into the company. Many immature business owners consume every penny of profit that they make, only to realize that they have no money left to restock their supplies. If the company provides services only, the owner discovers that service-related businesses must continually be updated (new programs, new services, etc.) to remain relevant.

9. **Laziness:** Let's face it. Some

entrepreneurs are just plain lazy. They have a "something for nothing" mindset. They'll build a non-professional website for themselves, fill the site with a bunch of non-professional photos and images and then, post the highest prices imaginable for whatever it is that they're selling. They won't update or market their websites. They'll just sit at their computers, wondering why no one is doing business with them. After this, they'll take to social media to rant about how they will never support any of their friends' businesses because no one supported their businesses.

10. **No Business Plan:** Write the vision and make it plain. Most believers know this scripture, but many business owners don't apply it to their businesses. For this reason, they cannot determine which direction they should be going on. Having a business plan in place helps you to check off the things that have been done and to

work on the things that need to be done.

Anytime a business is failing, there is a reason behind its failure. The business owner should examine the business and determine what he or she is doing wrong. An immature business owner will blame the failure of his or her business on people. They'll say things like, "People wouldn't support me because of jealousy," or "People kept taking advantage of me." These excuses are unfounded because, for example, if no one supports me because of jealously, it could only mean I'm marketing my products or services to the wrong crowd. More than likely, that crowd is familiar with me. Additionally, if someone keeps taking advantage of me, it's only because I let them do so. For me, I had to start doing the one thing I didn't want to do and that is ... be assertive and inflexible regarding how I do business. This meant that I had to learn to become comfortable offending people. Having been in business for seven years, I can say that I have offended many people, but

98% of my customers weren't offended when they walked away. They became repeat customers! The other two percent were people who tried to get past my posted rules and I wouldn't let them. Again, offending people is just a part of the business owner's life. I'm okay with it now, but there was a time when I hated disappointing people. If this is your mindset, it must change because there are people out there who won't mind disappointing you. Additionally, you should never set out to offend a customer intentionally. However, when you come across dominant, rule-hating customers who keep trying to over-talk you, those are customers you'll more than likely have to offend. Customers like that are bullies looking for someone to push around. For them, it's not about the services or products you provide; they are secondary. The customer simply is a power-thirsty soul who gets pleasure from delegating. When I get customers like these, I make them pay for the extra time, so if they want to be dominant and controlling, they have the right to be that way. However, I have the right to make them pay for the extra time they are requesting and this is always effective enough to drive them away.

Money Matters

In my book, *Christian & Entrepreneur: The Goal Mind to Success*, I interviewed a few business owners to see how much they'd invested into their businesses. What I found was that most business owners invest the equivalent of a high school kid's yearly allowance into their businesses. They then sit back and say things like, "As soon as my business takes off, I'm gonna invest more into it," not realizing that the money and time they have already invested in their businesses are what they've poured into those businesses as fuel. Your business will only go as far as you fuel it to go. Chanting inspirational, religious adages won't move your company because words without faith are fumes, just as faith without works is dead.

Establishing the Kingdom's culture or system within your business isn't just about investing in the business; it's about sowing seeds wherever God tells you to sow them. God does this so that we won't have wrongful relationships with money and material things. For example, there was a time when I renounced the first-fruits (tithe) doctrine because I'd read a lot of articles that said that tithing was an Old Testament practice. I couldn't find any evidence to refute this, plus, I didn't want my finances under the law (since the law does not justify, but condemns), so I stopped tithing. Did God bless me? Yes! He did and that's why I believed I was doing the right thing, but He blessed me because He loves me. He blessed me because I'd tapped into a system of blessings. However, I started buying a lot of things for myself. I ended up buying over 150 bottles of perfume and body sprays, plus, over 200 pairs of shoes. I bought a lot of costume jewelry and I started building a purse collection. This meant that I was beginning to have a wrongful relationship with my money and myself. When I joined my new church, I asked my Apostle about the tithing doctrine. I went to the meeting with an open mind, not determined to push my theology on him, but to hear what he had to say. In a few words, he managed to show me that God is a first-fruits kind of God. He said that Jesus, Himself, is a tithe. He helped me to understand the law of first-fruits. He didn't try to scare me into tithing; He just told me that God wants us to give Him the first-fruits of everything (our time, our days, our money) so that He can always be first on our minds. I suddenly remembered Matthew 6:33, which reads, "But seek first the Kingdom of God and his righteousness, and all these things will be added to you." I also remembered the times I'd fallen into the snares of idolatry, and in every one of those situations, I had not put God first. At that moment, my paradigm shifted. Ezekiel 36:26 (ESV) reads, "And I will give you a new heart, and a new spirit I will put within you. And I will remove the heart of stone from your flesh and give you a heart of flesh." I was in the midst of getting what the Word refers to as a new heart, which means to receive a new mind or a new system of thinking. As soon as I started tithing again, I became more selfless. I started looking for ways to bless people. I started thinking about things I should have been doing that I had not been doing (feeding the homeless, visiting the orphans, etc.) and I decided to make a change in my life. In other words, the old system was broken.

Many believers do not like to sow when they know they won't be receiving something in return. This is a consumer's mindset, and the average believer is bound by it and bound to it. Purchasing a new outfit is not sowing a seed. Think of it this way: you will reap an immediate harvest once the cashier hands you your bag and your receipt. However, there are seeds sown in faith; for example, you can give a meal to a homeless man and receive nothing (immediately) in exchange for giving him that meal. Because God is a God of sowing and reaping, He will bless you for the seed you've sown into that man over time; then again, the blessing may manifest in the lives of your children or your children's children. To sow into people who cannot give you an immediate harvest requires faith and love. Love will make you sow into a homeless man with no expectation of gain, but faith will serve as a reminder to you that you are a citizen of the Kingdom of God. As such, you are subject to the law of sowing and reaping, therefore, you can expect a harvest on the seed you've sown.

Another system of failure is found in impatience. Impatient people live under the policy of immediate return, which means that they expect an immediate return on every single one of their investments. For example, a business owner bound by this mentality could start a used car dealership, but he wouldn't be willing to finance the car through his company. This is because he wants an immediate return on his investment. This mentality will limit his company's success and eventually cause the failure of his company. After all, major car dealers may get the bulk of their money through financing. Some use bank financing, but others have gotten smart and started extending in-house financing to their customers. They realized that they were losing most of the money they could have made through bank financing. The bank decided that the risks involved with using your own funds is well worth it. Of course, we know that banks use the money we store up in them, but they are also backed by insurance. Insurance, for a bank, is not free. They pay for it as well, but again, they decided that it was worth the risk, since being an entrepreneur does involve a lot of risks.

Deuteronomy 28:12 (ESV): The Lord will open to you his good treasury, the heavens, to give the rain to your land in its season and to bless all the work of your hands. And you shall lend to many nations, but you shall not borrow.

One of the facets of lending is patience. Amazingly enough, patience is also one of the fruits of the Holy Spirit (see Galatians 5:22).

The more patient you are, the better the
return will be. Consider the parable of the
talents. Each man had been given one or
more talents and after their Master gave
them the talents, he left. Sometime later, the
master returned and gave each man his
reward. The guy who'd been given five
talents had doubled his talents. The guy
who'd been given two talents had also
doubled his talents. Notice that the reward
was not in the doubling of the talents; they
were simply excited to serve their master
through their talents. The guy who'd been
given one talent buried his and when the
master returned, he took the talent from the
guy and gave it to the more faithful servant.
He also threw the unfruitful servant in
prison. Prison can be used to represent
bondage.

More Than You Can Bear

My business was still relatively new and all I
had was $175 in my account. A man reached
out to me and began to minister to me. I
heard the Lord tell me to sow $100 into him.

Now, this made no sense to me because it would leave me with less than what I'd given the guy, but I honored God and did what He said. That same day, He told me to sow the remaining $75 into a woman I'd been following. Again, my natural mind did not want to do what God was telling me to do, but I knew not to reason with my natural mind. I obeyed God and not long after that, He expanded my business. He was simply testing my faith and getting me to put some seeds into the atmosphere so that He could give me a harvest.

This wasn't the only way I was tested. Earlier, I told you how God had me to close a hip hop site I'd built. After that, I renounced working for the world. There were times, after this new declaration, that I was the epitome of broke. It was during those times when some of the artists I used to work with would reach out to me, looking to hire me to design their websites. What's worse is, they'd be offering to pay me way more money than I needed. Nevertheless, I had to turn them away. Don't get me wrong — I'm glad I did because God has blessed me tremendously, but it wasn't always an easy decision to make, after all, I had material and non-material needs. It's not easy to turn away what you need, but you must remind yourself that you are choosing between fulfilling a temporary need versus trusting the Lord with your entire life.

There was another time when a woman had gone to my website and purchased one of the most expensive designs I had. I think it was over seven hundred bucks. When the order came through, I was excited, but then, she submitted the text that she wanted on the design. It was completely demonic, new age type of stuff. Disappointed, I logged into my PayPal account and hit refund. The point is, how you spend, make or invest money does matter to God. It shows Him where your heart is. In other words, it shows Him which realm or, better yet, kingdom, you are submitting yourself to.

Matthew 6:21 (ESV): For where your treasure is, there your heart will be also.

Matthew 25:23 (ESV): His master said to him, 'Well done, good and faithful servant. You have been faithful over a little; I will set you over much. Enter into the joy of your master.

The tests will come to see how much money and success you can handle. Some people can't handle more than $25,000 a year without getting prideful. God said, in 1 Corinthians 10:13, that He wouldn't put more on us than we can bear. Most people think this scripture is in reference to evil, but please understand that God does not bring evil upon us. What God is saying is that every vessel (person) has a capacity and He won't overfill that capacity if the vessel is not able to withstand the overflow without sinking into temptation (sin). So, if you can't go above making $25,000 a year without pride seeping in, you will continue to make $25,000 a year or less until you forsake pride and humble yourself. Therefore, some business owners can never seem to get past a certain point; they keep trying to expand their businesses, but not their minds. To continue expanding, the first thing we, as entrepreneurs, must do is examine ourselves thoroughly and we must do this daily. People who do not submit themselves to regular heart checkups eventually become prideful and unteachable. This means they'll become the people who draw near God with their mouths, even though their hearts are far from Him. This means that they will become individual kingdoms or vessels who are far away from God, even though they profess to be His sons and daughters.

There are some believers who can withstand an overflow of blessings because they've trusted God in all things. They are givers who do not serve money, but have, instead, learned to make money serve them. They are trustworthy believers who keep expanding their territories through godly submission. For these believers, God says that He will bless them beyond their capacity to receive. Of course, this means that God will grace the receivers to hold the blessings that He gives to them.

Malachi 3:10 (ESV): Bring the full tithe into the storehouse, that there may be food in my house. And thereby put me to the test, says the LORD of hosts, if I will not open the windows of heaven for you and pour down for you a blessing until there is no more need.

Luke 6:37-38 (ESV): Judge not, and you will not be judged; condemn not, and you will not be condemned; forgive, and you will be forgiven; give, and it will be given to you. Good measure, pressed down, shaken together, <u>running over</u>, will be put into your lap. For with the measure you use it will be measured back to you.

Understanding Strongholds

Earlier we talked about realms. Again, a realm is a royal domain or a kingdom. Most of us are also familiar with the term "stronghold," but in case you are not, a stronghold can be both natural (military, fortress, etc.) and soulish (against the mind, will and emotions). Google defines the word "stronghold" two ways and they are:

1. A place that has been fortified to protect it against attack.
2. A place where a particular cause or belief is strongly defended or upheld.

A stronghold can also be when an opposing military encamps around a land, region or country. By doing so, the army ensures that no one can leave that place, nor can anyone enter it. This stops the country or region under attack from trading with the lands they have trade agreements with. Eventually, famine starts to set in and the country becomes weaker and more susceptible to an attack.

A stronghold of the mind occurs when a person believes something so strongly that he or she is unwilling, and sometimes unable, to receive any information that contradicts what he or she believes. This stronghold can be self-imposed through the lack of knowledge, coupled with the abundance of pride or it can be demonic. Additionally, a good stronghold of the mind is when a believer is fortified by the Word of God. The

Lord calls such a believer "blessed," meaning that believer has been supernaturally endowed with power from on high.

Psalms 1:1-4 (ESV): Blessed is the man who walks not in the counsel of the wicked, nor stands in the way of sinners, nor sits in the seat of scoffers; but his delight is in the law of the Lord,
and on his law, he meditates day and night. He is like a tree planted by streams of water that yields its fruit in its season, and its leaf does not wither. In all that he does, he prospers. The wicked are not so, but are like chaff that the wind drives away.

In every stronghold, there is a strongman. Merriam Webster's online dictionary defines the word "strongman" as: *one who leads or controls by force of will and character or by military methods.* In military terms, it is the ruler over a militant group; it is the person who passes down the orders, the person who has the greatest authority. A demonic strongman is the commander over a certain unit of demons. For example, in deliverance, you will often witness the minister saying, "I bind the strongman," or he may call the demon out by name. The spirit of rejection is a common strongman and it rules over every other demonic force that has encamped against the soul of a believer. Lastly, when we are submitted to the Lord, Jesus can be the strongman of our lives if we allow Him to take His place in our hearts. Remember, we are talking about the stronghold of the mind. Believe it or not, the strongman will determine what you do with and how you treat your money. Basically, the strongman is the one who determines how you spend or invest your money. If Jesus is your strongman, you will be a faithful tither and giver. You will help the homeless and be led by the Spirit of God in relation to how to sow back into the Kingdom of God. If Mammon is your strongman, you will sow into his kingdom. You will support ungodly musicians, be driven by selfish ambition and misuse people to get what you want. Under the Mammon principality, people tend to erect themselves as idols, with money being their highest idol. Under Mammon, people knowingly and unknowingly practice polytheism, which is the belief in and worship of many gods.

The love of money is a realm; it is a kingdom within itself. It is a stronghold designed to interrupt and pervert a believer's communication with God, thereby, controlling the believer's finances. Again, this kingdom is run by the principality Mammon and it has claimed more lives, peace and inheritances than any other realm or principality. Mammon literally teaches believers how to access the gifts that God has placed within them, and then, pervert those gifts by submitting them to the kingdom of darkness. People under Mammon's headship are infatuated with power, money and fame — so much so that they chase these things more than they chase God. They want recognition, they want validation and they want to be worshiped.

1 Timothy 6:10 (ESV): For the love of money is a root of all kinds of evils. It is through this craving that some have wandered away from the faith and pierced themselves with many pangs.

Matthew 6:24 (ESV): No one can serve two masters, for either he will hate the one and love the other, or he will be devoted to the one and despise the other. You cannot serve God and money.

People often justify staying under Mammon's kingdom by saying things like:

"The pastor just wants my money!"

"He or she (the pastor) can get a job, just like I got a job!"

"God knows my heart."

"God don't need my money! The Bible says that the Earth is the Lord's and the fullness thereof!"

"Let him who is without sin, cast the first stone."

In other words, people often memorize and misinterpret scriptures to justify staying bound. Mammon convinces believers that they can and should put themselves first and then, give God what's left. The problem is, once we begin to consume our seeds, we rarely and barely leave anything behind. So, people are bound for generation upon generation by the spirit of lack. Understand this, lack and poverty are both spirits under Mammon's rule. Poverty is oftentimes a ruling spirit or lower level principality under the principality of Mammon.

The point is, in your business dealings, you want to make sure that you are submitted to God in the area of your finances, just as you are submitted to Him in every other area of your life. The Bible tells us to not give place to the devil, meaning, do not give an opportunity or occasion to the devil. He will not waste an opportunity to bring you into subjection to himself. He will not waste an opportunity to attack you. Make sure the strongman of your life is Jesus Christ, Himself. If the realm of thinking you're in does not line up with the Word of God, renounce that realm, close that door and shift your paradigm to another realm. You do this by reading and believing the Word of God. Remember, in every kingdom, there is a system: a way in which things are done. If you are unsure of what kingdom you are serving, not just with lip service, but through actual servitude, look at the fruit in your life and re-examine your daily system. Do not be bound by a consumer's mindset, because consumers only pay for the solutions to problems, thus, creating more demand (problems) for solution-minded people to fulfill. This means that solution-minded people get richer, while consumers get hungrier, work harder and spend more.

Lastly, people under poverty's rule have a system that repeatedly dries up their finances. Having grown up in poverty and around a lot of poverty-minded people, I got a chance to see poverty in action.

Poverty-minded people submit themselves to the United States government, any entity, and any person who is willing to supply their needs. They will agree to stay in the roughest neighborhoods, work the worst jobs, spend many days without necessities — all in exchange for food, housing and supplies. I grew up around people who would not get a traditional job, out of fear that they'd lose their government assistance. I've literally seen family members quit their jobs because the government cut off or lowered their relief. Additionally, poverty-minded people can only make a certain amount of money weekly, bi-weekly, monthly and annually without losing their peace. Again, I've seen this in operation. When a person bound by poverty receives more money than he or she is accustomed to receiving, that person will lose his or her peace and shop until the money is gone or is right back in the range that he or she is accustomed to having. Consider income tax season. When a person bound by poverty receives his or her taxes, that person will take off work and shop until he or she is almost broke. People under the government of poverty will finance cars that they can barely afford, and a few months to a year later, they'll be hiding those cars from the repo man. People under poverty's rule will spend hundreds of dollars on name brand clothes, all the while, letting their monthly utilities go unpaid for months at a time. People under poverty's rule will spend their children's lunch money getting their hair and nails done. This isn't to insult you if this has been your lifestyle; it is to help you to see the system that you are under. That way, you will know who you've been blindly serving. Once we realize the systems that we are under, we are then empowered to break those systems.

Money matters. If it matters to us, it matters to God. Sure, God doesn't need our money; He wants our cooperation. He is teaching us to think and behave like Him; that way, His Kingdom can be established here on Earth. Remember this, God gave us dominion over the Earth. Dominion is a system He established in the Earth and God will never violate His own systems. Whatever He has established, it is established and cannot be undone. This means the King of kings will consult with us (the kings and queens) regarding the systems that we are imploring. If our systems do not align with His systems, He recognizes that we are not submitted to His Kingdom, even if we claim to be.

However, when our systems align with His, we will begin to experience Heaven on Earth. You have dominion (governing authority); use it wisely.

Genesis 1:26 (ESV): Then God said, "Let us make man in our image, after our likeness. And let them have dominion over the fish of the sea and over the birds of the heavens and over the livestock and over all the earth and over every creeping thing that creeps on the Earth."

Luke 10:19 (ESV): Behold, I have given you authority to tread on serpents and scorpions, and over all the power of the enemy, and nothing shall hurt you.

The Faith to Invest

Let's face it. Some believers are unbelievably frugal. What I've come to notice is that frugal people often think they are making wise decisions with their money and this isn't always true. Frugality oftentimes causes people to spend more money than they should have (in the long run) and make a whole lot of bad decisions. The reason is, a lot of frugality is centered around fear. Fear gives birth to self-coddling and self-pity which, in turn, gives birth to self-righteousness. Remember this: we are living vessels designed by God, and we all have a capacity. Frugal people are like large ships filled with goods, but the captains of those ships are too afraid to trade with anyone. Instead, the captains start behaving like pirates, manipulating and stealing from any ship they find within their reach.

Oftentimes, I'll get an order from an

extremely frugal customer. Now, understand this — just because the person is cheap doesn't mean that he or she doesn't have any money. The reality is, some people have an "end of the world" mentality. They are not preparing for Armageddon. All too often, the problem is, they've suffered through a lot of lack in their lives to the point where they have been traumatized by that lack. They fear not having enough, so they become manipulative in their attempts to save every penny they can save. They are the ones who will go to a hot tamale stand and hold up the line. You'll hear them saying things like, "Aw, come on. Eight dollars for hot tamales?! The guy up the street sells his for five bucks and that's all I have on me right now is five bucks!" They won't necessarily be mean to the guy, but they will hold up the line, cost him a few customers and do whatever they can do to manipulate him into lowering his prices. This Armageddon mentality is centered around their fear of some sudden, unexpected tragedy that they won't be able to weather.

You won't find anyone more desperate and dangerous than a traumatized prophet. Traumatized prophets hear from God, but because they live in fear, they try to sell the Word, instead of releasing it. This is why it is necessary for us to get the healing we need before attempting to start businesses. If we don't, whatever traumas we've suffered will bleed over into our businesses and our ministries. It will affect how we do business, who we do business with and how long our companies stay in business. Consequentially, we will develop systems for our businesses that will be built on the foundations of our traumatic experiences. This means that our businesses would not have secure foundations; instead, they'll be built on our emotions and fears.

Many traumatized prophets are afraid to invest in their businesses. They say things like:

> "I'm saving for a rainy day."
> "Once my business starts generating more funds, I'll invest more into it."

"I invested one time and got burned."

Business, just like life, has many risks that you'll take, but it won't fail unless you become loss-focused, rather than solution-oriented. You must learn from each loss; this will help you to fortify your business and not make the same mistakes you once made. You will make mistakes; that's inevitable, but you don't give up because of them. You learn from them.

People who don't invest in their businesses are people who aren't willing to take risks. This is self-sabotage at its best. For example, I've been in failed relationships, failed friendships and had failed business dealings, but I won't let any of these make me afraid of having relationships and friendships with other people, nor will I shut my business down. To grow, I had to learn from those experiences, instead of letting them imprison me in fear or define me. This means I had to continue taking risks because risks are a part of life. They are also a part of business ownership.

Just as you will make sound business decisions, there will be times when the decisions you make aren't so sound. This is normal; these are the ups and downs of entrepreneurship. I've had ideas that I've invested in, only for them to flop. I've also had ideas that were very fruitful. The point is, I was willing to invest, even though I didn't know what the outcome would be. Some people would focus on the money lost on failed ideas, but successful entrepreneurs don't lose anything. Instead, we collect the wisdom behind each failure.

Let's take authorship, for example. There are a lot of believers out there who God has instructed to write books. He's given them the topics and the time to complete their literary assignments, but they keep spending that time making excuses. The reality is, authors are entrepreneurs. They own books and they get paid royalties on those books. They even have to file taxes on the royalties they receive, but before they became authors, they had to invest. They had to pay for editing, pay to get their book covers designed and pay to have their books published. Some have even paid for book trailers, press kits and other forms of branding. Investing is sowing seeds. Then again, there are many, many believers out there who will throw a book together, use a free program to create a low budget cover for themselves and use a free program to publish their books. So, they end up giving birth to something that has not been properly sown into, and for this reason, their books are full of spelling and grammatical errors, plus, they aren't formatted properly. Their book covers look atrocious or they are common templates that other authors use. This costs authors 80 to 90 percent of the sales that they could have made on their books if they'd just trusted God. I teach a writer's class and one thing I often warn the students about is desiring to be an author so badly that they miss the opportunity to become best-sellers. Some people get the "author" title and that's all they want. Of course, this line of reasoning is oftentimes centered around rejection and the need to feel validated by others. Others invest large amounts of money and time into their books because the author title to them is secondary. What's first, for them, is obeying God and giving birth to a product that God wouldn't mind co-signing.

Your investment will always match your faith. It is a representation of how much you know about God, how much you trust Him and how much you love Him. Consider the parable of the talents.

Matthew 25:14-30 (ESV): For it will be like a man going on a journey, who called his servants and entrusted to them his property. To one he gave five talents, to another two, to another one, to each according to his ability. Then he went away. He who had received the five talents went at once and traded with them, and he made five talents more. So he who had the two talents made two talents more. But he who had received the one talent went and dug in the ground and hid his master's money. Now after a long time the master of those servants came and settled accounts with them. And he who had received the five talents came forward, bringing five talents more, saying, "Master, you delivered to me five talents; here, I have made five talents more." His master said to him, "Well done, good and faithful servant. You have been faithful over a little; I will set you over much. Enter into the joy of your master." And he also who had the two talents came forward, saying, "Master, you delivered to me two talents; here, I have made two talents more." His master said to him, "Well done, good and faithful servant. You have been faithful over a little; I will set you over much. Enter into the joy of your master." He also who had received the one talent came forward, saying, "Master, I knew you to be a hard man, reaping where you did not sow, and gathering where you scattered no seed, so I was afraid, and I went and hid your talent in the ground. Here, you have what is yours." But his master answered him, "You wicked and slothful servant! You knew that I reap where I have not sown and gather where I scattered no seed? Then you ought to have invested my money with the bankers, and at my coming I should have received what was my own with interest. So take the talent from him and give it to him who has the ten talents. For to everyone who has will more be given, and he will have an abundance. But from the one who has not, even what he has will be taken away. And cast the worthless servant into the outer darkness. In that place there will be weeping and gnashing of teeth."

In this parable, we see that the master gave every one of his servants a certain number of talents, meaning, they all had talents. There wasn't a single servant who did not possess a talent. The same is true for us today.

The one He'd given five talents to went out and doubled what He'd give him. He didn't make excuses, nor did he question why he had a greater responsibility than the other servants, after all, to whom much is given, much is required. The one who was given two talents could have griped as well. Why did his fellow servant receive five talents? Instead of griping, he went out and doubled what he'd received. Finally, the slothful servant had received one talent, obviously because he couldn't be trusted with more. It was all that he could bear. He took that one talent and buried it in the ground. When confronted by his master, he started pointing the fingers of blame at the master, saying, "I've always known you to be a hard man. You reap where you have not sown. You gather fruit in places where you haven't sown any seeds." This means that his view of his master was warped. He saw his master as a wicked man, and for this reason, he didn't want to help him prosper. He decided to bury the talent the master had given him, just so he could hand it back to him upon his return. The other servants doubled what the master had given them, but the slothful servant was double-minded. On one hand, he was a servant, but on the other hand, it was clear that he despised the one in which he served.

How many of us believers are doing this right now?

Many believers won't invest in the businesses God has given them because they don't feel like He is a good God. They won't say this aloud, but it's in their hearts. They'd rather work a nine to five than to prosper the Kingdom of God. They call themselves servants of the Most High God and they'll come to church every Sunday, but they do not and will not serve God. When they do start businesses, their companies are the equivalent of stopped up liquid soap testers, meaning, they have not invested the time and money needed into prospering their businesses. For this reason, they are testing the market, but not flowing in it.

Giving

Anyone can start a business, but there aren't many people who can maintain their businesses. This is because a lot of believers don't have a heart for giving. If you have trouble giving in church, you'll have trouble investing in your business. Again, this is oftentimes due to fear, a lack of knowledge, misconceptions about leadership and self-worship. Understand this: we must exercise giving before we become comfortable with it. It's a wise idea to find good ground to sow into and use that ground to practice your giving.

Sowing

In business, you will have to sow repeatedly. There will be times when you've made, for example, $800 on an order, only to have to put that entire amount back into your business. You'll have to pay for hosting your website, flyers, toll-free numbers, programs or products to enhance your services and so on. If you do not upgrade your services or products, you will get left behind. Entrepreneurship is continuous giving, therefore, you need to practice giving to others. You can practice giving at homeless shelters or sending money to missionary programs that help starving children. Find somewhere to sow and start sowing. Start by sowing outside of your comfort zone. What you are doing is fighting against any ungodly relationship with money that you have. What you are doing is dismantling fear and taking God at His Word.

A woman once reached out to me and asked me if I would publish her book for free. Of course, I told her no. She went on and on about how she was going to pray for God to touch my heart in the matter. I asked the woman, "Why don't you ask God to touch your wallet? Why don't you ask Him to give you the money you need to pay for your publishing, instead of asking Him to touch my heart?" She started stuttering. She said, "I'm just gonna pray for Him to touch your heart." I kept asking why, but then, the Lord answered me. It was because she could not be trusted with the money and she knew this. If God had given it to her, she would have swallowed it whole. God never impressed upon my heart to sow my services or time into that woman's book because her book was and is her responsibility. God will never give you a vision without giving you provision; He will never give you an assignment without giving you the ability to complete that assignment. You may look into your bank account and notice that you don't have the money today to do whatever it is that He's told you to do, but if you decide within your heart to do it, He will provide the people, money and time you'll need to obey Him. Sometimes, He does this at the last minute. However, He won't tell you to write a book or start a business without giving you the provision to write that book or run that business. We just have to be willing to sow the seeds, instead of ingesting them.

The Free Dictionary by Farlex gives us an extended definition of the word "invest." It defines "invest" this way:

1. To commit (money or capital) in order to gain a financial return.
2. To spend or devote for future advantage or benefit: invested much time and energy in getting a. good education.

   b. To devote morally or psychologically, as to a purpose; commit.
3.   To endow with authority or power.
Let's look at each individual definition.

To commit (money or capital) in order to gain a financial return: The word "invest" is the corporate word for "sow." It is often used in reference to money, even though it can be used outside of the financial arena. For example, we can invest our time into something or someone. When we invest money, we can expect a financial return as well as a return on whatever it is that we've sown into. For example, if we sow into a prophet, we will reap what the Bible calls a prophet's reward.

To spend or devote for future advantage or benefit: This definition is a little off because it uses the word "spend." Anything spent yields an immediate return; for example, if I purchase a pack of gum, the cashier will bag the gum up and hand it to me. In this scenario, I've spent money to receive something. This means that I have my reward. If I order something from online, I will have to wait for it to be shipped, nevertheless, the money is still spent because I'm exchanging it for something tangible. The correct word is "invest." When we invest, whether that seed be our time, ideas or money, we have sown into something intangible (in most cases). The return you receive on a seed won't always be something your five senses can engage with. The most valuable return on a seed is a greater capacity of faith. Some people have faith the size of a mustard seed and the Bible tells us that this is all that is needed to move a mountain. Then again, there are people who have mountain-sized faith and these people have the ability to become incubators for those mustard seeds to grow in and produce mustard trees. These mustard trees grow up and release more seeds which, in turn, become more tress. The point is, faith comes in different sizes.

Romans 12:3 (ESV): For by the grace given to me I say to everyone among you not to think of himself more highly than he ought to think, but to think with sober judgment, each according to the measure of faith that God has assigned.

To endow with authority or power: It's amazing that this particular definition was taken from a secular dictionary, but it is true. Whatever you invest into, you empower. For example, if you open a bank account, you are empowering your bank to stay in business. If you invest your time into gossip, you are empowering the words spoken in gossip to go forth and do whatever it is that the enemy wants them to do. If you invest your time into worrying, you empower the evil that is contending with your faith. If you invest your money and time into your business, you empower your business to succeed.

As a prophetic entrepreneur, you need to stay completely in tune with the heart of God. The reason is, the enemy loves to develop strategies to attack Kingdom businesses and sometimes, he will find legal grounds to do so. However, when we submit our hearing and our hearts to God, He will tell us when we are out of order or when we need to switch directions. A lot of marketplace ministers have lost their businesses because they allowed fear, selfish ambition and lack to drive them right into one of the devil's many traps. For example, the Lord told them to invest in a program or to stop investing in a person, but they did not listen. As a result, the warfare they experienced was not strong enough to kill them, but it was strong enough to destroy their businesses.

Faithless with Works

The Bible tells us that faith without works is dead, but what about faithlessness with works? One of the hardest things to do is invest in something you don't believe in. Amazingly enough, many believers will invest in business ideas and strategies that they have absolutely no faith in. So, what compelled them to invest? They met someone who inspired them to do so. Inspiration can easily ensnare a marketplace minister who does not have faith in the assignment God has given him or her.

There are people out there who can recharge your faith in a matter of minutes. A simple conversation with one of these people will have you ready to write every book, start every business and work on every invention that the Lord has given you. Once you go out of their presence, you'll still have the residue of their anointing on your heart. This is usually when most people get excited and start paying for their branding and doing whatever they know to be necessary to start their businesses. However, that residue is a seed that must be maintained, meaning, the person in question must go deeper in their relationship with God. They must bury their flesh for the seeds in them to grow. The average believer refuses to die to self, and therefore, experiences something similar to a caffeine crash. They are momentarily energized and ready to take the world, but eventually, that excitement wears off when it's not being cultivated.

I was driving home from church one day when I looked up at my GPS system. I know my way home from church, so it wasn't giving me directions at that time, but it still displayed the number of minutes I had before I reached my house. It listed eight minutes as my estimated time of arrival. I thought to myself, what if someone who lacked understanding were to stop at that very moment while their GPS systems displayed "eight minutes?" What if they were to stop and wait eight, nine or ten minutes? Would they be silly enough to sue the manufacturers of the GPS system, arguing that the system said they'd be home in eight minutes, instead, eight minutes later, they were still in the same spot? Of course, we live in a time when someone would be silly enough to do this. The point is, even though the GPS system said I had eight minutes before I arrived at my house, I still had to drive. I still had to do the work.

Just as there is faith without works, there are faithless works. A good example would be a mother driving her daughter to the cheerleader tryouts, even though she doesn't believe her daughter will make the team. Another example would be a man who buys a nicotine patch to help him stop smoking, along with a carton of cigarettes. These are faithless works. Many marketplace prophets operate in this very same way. They hear prophetic words from Heaven, sow into those words and then sit around, waiting to see "if" they'll come to pass, rather than believing that they have already come to pass. These are spiritual gamblers who eventually lose their faith because they keep giving Satan the upper hand.

Investing Time & Etiquette

When I worked in secular America, I was rarely ever late for work. I learned my work etiquette from my mother. She worked hard and the only time she called in was when she was really sick. Most of the time, the doctor had to tell her to stay home.

I worked full time for around fifteen years. I

started my business while working full time as a 411 operator. I would come home from work and go straight to working for myself, even when I didn't have any orders. At that time, I was running a hip hop website, plus, I designed websites for artists.

While working my business, I partnered with a friend of mine which turned out to be a mistake. I offered assignments to other friends and people I've met and one thing I came to learn was, there are some lazy people out there.

One of the reputations I've garnered is that I work quick. Honestly, I've spoiled my customers, so if I say the project will take three days, they don't believe me. If it's not done in a matter of 12-24 hours, I'll get inundated with calls and emails. Of course, this is a good problem to have — sometimes. Nevertheless, I met a young woman who was unemployed. I told her about the type of work I did and she said that she could edit text well. She said she'd done this for a few people, so when I got a customer who needed content for his website, I thought of her because I had too many orders to complete his order within his time-frame. He would be paying $150 for me to write seven pages of text for his website (about us, bio, home page intro, etc.). The job seemed easy and I wanted to be a blessing to her, so I offered the job to her. I would accept the cash and send it, along with the order details, to her. The customer kept insisting that he wanted me to work on his project, but he wasn't willing to give me any leeway regarding his time-frame. I reassured him that she was a professional and she would do the job right. I told him that if he didn't like her work, I'd come back and redo it at no extra charge. He reluctantly agreed. He sent me the money and I made the mistake of sending it, along with the order instructions, to the young woman.

Now, normally, if I had done the project, I would have finished it in a day's time, but I would have told him that I needed a week. That way, if anything slowed me down, I wouldn't be overwhelmed.

It was three weeks later and I was talking with the young woman over the phone. I asked her if she'd finished the guy's project and she said no. She told me how they had gotten into a mild argument over it and he'd said to her, "I'm gonna tell Tiffany." She told me that she'd responded, "Well, tell Tiffany. What is she gonna do to me? I'm grown." I couldn't believe what I was hearing. She'd pocketed the $150 bucks, insulted my customer and never finished the work.

I hired another friend some time after that. She too was unemployed. I hired her to edit a customer's book for me because the book needed what we (editors) call a hard edit. Honestly, it needed to be rewritten. I asked her if she wanted the project and she said yes. Because I knew that she needed the money, I sent it right away. She took a lot longer than necessary editing the book and she complained the entire time about how poorly it was written. When she finally sent it over, I noticed that she'd skipped pages, meaning, there were some pages she didn't bother editing. Additionally, I could see where she'd gotten frustrated and had given up. I noticed that she'd struck out paragraphs and paragraphs of text and she'd even started ignoring a lot of the mistakes she'd come across. She stopped editing at some point and started correcting a few mistakes here and there to make it look like she'd edited the book when she hadn't. I had to go back through that entire book and re-edit it. Like the other girl, she wanted to start her own business doing much of what I did, but they lacked the work etiquette needed to perform in this industry. They saw the fruit of my labor, but they not want to assume the responsibility or endure the process needed to grow fruit for themselves.

If you are going to start a business, you must be willing to make sacrifices. Your reputation isn't just built upon how good your products and services are; it is centered around your attitude and your timeline to completion.

Understand this, a customer would much rather pay more money to someone who works and behaves professionally than they would with someone who just works. There have been many, many nights where I craved sleep, but I had orders to complete. I had to get up, walk around and collect myself so that I could honor my word to my customers. I remember people talking about new hit shows and playing the newest games, but every Thursday while they were being entertained, I was working. I've never seen the majority, if any, of the hit shows that everyone was talking about from 2012-2016. I was too busy to be bound to a television set. Let me explain why.

One thing I tell most marketplace ministers is that prophetic people tend to have pit-bull tenacity, meaning, once we start something, it's hard for us to stop it. I recognized this in myself a long time ago. For this reason, I realized that I had to tame that part of me. I needed to be careful what I locked in on. I knew that if I played games like Candy Crush,

I would get addicted and waste a whole lot of time entertaining myself, so I stayed away from it altogether. I also knew that if I started watching those daily or weekly shows that most people were being mesmerized by, I'd join the best of them. For this reason, I channeled my pit-bull tenacity into my relationship with God and building my brand. I purchased hundreds of notebooks, wrote out many strategies and gave birth to many products and services. I learned to avoid entertaining fruitless hobbies. The one thing I made the mistake of doing during that time was allowing a couple of idle people to take up a lot of my time.

Always remember this: if you are prophetic, you are tenacious. Do not waste your time being entertained by someone else's creativity when you have your own. Every time you sit down in front of a television set or a computer, you are making an investment. You are investing your time and cable dollars into another person's work. Understand this, there is a difference between an entertainer versus the entertained. Sure, you may not be an entertainer, but you should be a diligent worker, meaning, you shouldn't waste precious moments being entertained when you could have been building, researching, or strategizing. There's nothing wrong with being occasionally entertained, but you don't want to make this a part of your system. You work almost every day because you have bills that must be paid. Your business will need you to be as tenacious as you are (or were) on your secular job. You can't take time off just because you want to be entertained. Honestly, you need to be more diligent with your own business than you were with another man's business. Always remember that there is a difference between spent time versus invested time. There is an immediate, not-so-valuable return on spent time, but invested time produces a harvest that supernaturally increases over time.

How to Invest (Sow)

I would be remiss to tell you about the many

problematic mindsets that people have, without telling you how to get past those mindsets.

How do you receive the heart of an entrepreneur? You do this one seed at a time. I know that this may sound contradictory, but you should still sow when you do not have the faith to sow. A few paragraphs ago, I told you about people who receive a word and then wait to see "if" God will bring that word to pass, and I called them gamblers. So, how is this different? It's simple: you don't just sow a seed and wait. You must turn the ground! What does this mean? If you're believing God for a new car, for example, and He told you to sow a sizable seed at church, you need to obey Him. Also understand the warfare that will come behind that obedience. Warfare isn't always a physical attack; it can be mental. So, you may start wrestling with the spirit of worry. That demon may say to you, "Now, how are you going to pay your car note?" In this moment, you must act like Abram when he fought the birds of prey off his offering.

Genesis 15:7-11 (ESV): And he said to him, "I am the LORD who brought you out from Ur of the Chaldeans to give you this land to possess." But he said, "O Lord GOD, how am I to know that I shall possess it?" He said to him, "Bring me a heifer three years old, a female goat three years old, a ram three years old, a turtledove, and a young pigeon." And he brought him all these, cut them in half, and laid each half over against the other. But he did not cut the birds in half. And when birds of prey came down on the carcasses, Abram drove them away.

When worry and doubt contend with whatever the Lord has said to you, you must cast those thoughts down, bind up the spirits and drive them away from you.

2 Corinthians 10:5-6 (KJV): Casting down imaginations, and every high thing that exalteth itself against the knowledge of God, and bringing into captivity every thought to the obedience of Christ; and having in a readiness to revenge all disobedience, when your obedience is fulfilled.

Below are four tips to investing.
1. **Fast and pray:** Fasting and prayer helps you to hear from God; that way, you don't make any bad investments. Sometimes, good ideas are not God ideas and that's why we shouldn't be led by our understanding or our emotions in business dealings.
2. **Find good ground and sow into it:** Again, be prayerful because it is possible to sow into bad ground with good intentions. Your church home is a great place to start sowing if, of course, God led you there. Orphanages and nursing homes are also fertile grounds to sow into.
3. **Fight off the birds of prey:** The birds of prey are always demons, but they'll use any "body" they can use. For example, after sowing a seed, someone may call and offend you. The goal is to not get offended, but to bless them instead. Let's say, for example, that one

of your siblings suddenly called you and started accusing you of talking about them. Now, you haven't said anything to anyone about that sibling, so you try to defend yourself, but your sibling refuses to calm down. He or she starts unleashing a fury of words on you, and now, you feel your flesh waking up. What's the correct response to such a situation? Fight the birds of prey off your offering! You don't wait for the birds to land before you start swatting at them. You fan them away the moment you see them coming. So, if faced with a contentious sibling, you would simply need to say, "I haven't said anything about you." After that, you should not sit on the phone and listen to that sibling continue on about the matter. You've already resolved it, so the correct response is to apologize for any misunderstanding and if he or she refuses to calm down, you should hang up. What you're doing is refusing to let their anger become your anger. You are fighting off the birds of prey.

4. **Go and possess the land: God** would often tell Israel to "go and possess the land," even though the inhabitants of that land were still living and thriving in it. God first declared that He was giving the land to the Israelites. This meant that the inhabitants suddenly became illegal squatters on the land, meaning, Israel had the right to the land in question. It was theirs for the taking. The same is true of you. Whatever God has promised you, it is yours for the taking. You just must go and possess it, meaning, if you are planning to rent a particular building, you should contact the landlord of that business, even though you don't have the money to get started. In every war they fought, the Israelites didn't have enough manpower or resources to overcome their enemies, but every time they trusted God, they came out victorious.

Spies in the Land

"The LORD spoke to Moses, saying, 'Send men to spy out the land of Canaan, which I am giving to the people of Israel. From each tribe of their fathers you shall send a man, every one a chief among them'" (Numbers 13:1) ESV.

Why did the Sovereign, all-knowing God tell Moses to send spies to Canaan, when He is omnipresent? He knew everything that took place in Canaan. He knew when a blade of grass was cut and when a gust of wind blew through that nation. So, why did God have Moses to utilize spies? The answer is simple: it was to build the people's faith. They needed to know who they were up against; that way, when God defeated their enemies, they could give Him the glory.

When the spies came back, they spoke of the great things that were in the land, but they also spoke of the giants on the land. They incited fear in the heart of the people. This was not okay with God, but still, it did give Him the opportunity He wanted to show Himself powerful.

Just like God instructed Moses to send spies to Canaan, we must understand that our enemy, Satan, sends people to spy into our lives. These people come in the forms of family members, friends, and sometimes, fellow servants of the Lord. They aren't' people who are bowed down at the altar of Satan, receiving instructions from hell. These are oftentimes broken, blinded by sin, well-meaning, religious people who can't seem to see past themselves. They work tirelessly to establish soul ties (kingdom ties) with other believers so they can get a closeup look into their lives. If they see fruit that they want to take for themselves, they will use flattery, fear or scriptures in their attempts to get what they want. One such spy is called a time-waster.

The Time Waster

A time-waster is oftentimes a person who gets close enough to other people and then, starts wasting their time. For example, let's say that you are a successful business woman. You have a growing business and you are at peace in your life. God has clearly showered His favor upon you. A woman notices how favored you are and decides within her heart that she wants to be your best friend, not because she likes you, but because she wants what's on your life. Nevertheless, she's lazy. You work countless hours each day, seven days a week to get what you have, but she spends most of her time watching television. However, she wants every blessing that God has given to you, meaning, she is wrestling with jealousy, but because she doesn't feel spiteful towards you, she doesn't know that she's entertaining the spirit of jealousy.

One day, you give that woman your phone number and just like most new friendships, the first conversation lasts for several hours.

After that conversation, she says, "Girl, we are gonna have to do this again soon! You have truly blessed me! I've told you stuff that I've never told anyone. I don't know why, but I just feel super comfortable around you!" That's flattery, of course. A couple of days later, she calls you again, but this time, she listens more and asks you more personal questions about yourself. She seems genuinely interested in becoming your friend, so you let your guard down. Two weeks later, she says those infamous words, "You are my best friend." You're not feeling it, but you say it anyway. "You're my best friend too." From that point on, she starts calling you more often and the compliments never seem to end. Before long, you're talking on the phone with her every day, several hours at a time. Now, instead of her becoming as busy as you are, you are now becoming as wasteful with your time as she is with hers. This is because you are now in the grips of a time-waster.

A time-waster is oftentimes a person who

has nothing better to do with his or her time than to waste other people's time. They will call you just to tell you how hot it is outside, what they've had for lunch and how it tasted. They will magnify small issues in their lives, get overly emotional about those issues, and then, want you to spend hours trying to calm them down. A good example would be if their boss didn't speak to them at work earlier. They will inundate you with phone calls, talking about how hard they've worked, how dedicated they've been and who they believe has gotten into their manager's ears. Even when you silence their fears with facts, they will keep talking until your phone's battery gives out. If their phone's battery dies, they'll plug it up and call you right back.

A time-waster is one of the most common enemies that Christian entrepreneurs get ensnared by. This is because we need our time to build our businesses, hear from God and strategize. If a time-waster lives near you, that person will repeatedly show up at your house unannounced. If one does not live near you, he or she will call you whenever there is a shift in their emotions. If they're angry, they'll call you. If they're excited, they'll call you. If they're bored, they'll call you. If they are sleepy, they'll call you. If they've got indigestion, they'll call you. The point is, a time waster will waste your time in the same manner they waste their own.

Time-wasters hate to think with their own brains; they need the validation of others, so they will call you, for example, while they are shopping. They'll say things like, "I like these shoes, but I don't know if I should get them. They'd look good with my brown slacks, but I don't want to spend that kind of money." After that, they'll pause to hear your response to the conversation they'd just had with themselves. Again, this is because they don't like to make decisions for themselves by themselves. Then again, many time-wasters will use your time but never follow your advice. They simply wanted an extra head to think with and another voice to contend with. They wanted you to play the bad cop and say no, so they could play the good cop and tell themselves yes.

We tend to give time-wasters the majority of our time because they often label us as friends or best friends. One of the things every person who desires to run a (successful) business should know is this ... you can't afford to have needy people in your life because they'll need the very same things that your business needs and that is your time, resources and emotional strength. Often referred to by many as vampire spirits, time-wasting demons want to drain you so that you won't be able to fulfill your God-given assignment.

Jezebel

In business, one of the most common spirits you will encounter is the Jezebel spirit. This is because when you tap into the entrepreneur from within, you have simultaneously tapped into the prophetic realm. Of course, Jezebel is attracted to the prophets of God, but not in a good way. That spirit wants to usurp God's authority and it does this by using the spirits of control and mind control to do its evil beckoning.

Like many prophetic entrepreneurs, my journey started with no formal training from anyone. I learned through trial and error. I also learned by simply listening to the Holy Spirit, but the truth is, I wouldn't always listen to Him. You see, if God tells you to take your prices up, for example, when you know that you haven't been getting many orders to start with, you start reasoning with your intellect. Because God's request doesn't make sense to you, you will likely reason that you did not hear from God. This was my story.

It was around 2012 and I was charging $75 to custom create seals and logos for ministries. At that time, I kept getting the worst customers I'd ever worked with. I'd started putting some rules in place, but because I charged far too little for my services, I would bend those rules quite often out of fear that I'd lose the few orders I got monthly. I was miserable. A lot of my customers were taking advantage of me; I felt like people were holding the money they owed me over my head and making me leap repeatedly for it. I'd even considered walking away from graphic design altogether because I was becoming weary. The Lord kept telling me to take my prices up, but I wouldn't listen.

The type of people I kept attracting seemed to grow worse. To make matters worse, the most manipulative and condescending customers I had would refer their controlling, manipulative and condescending friends to me. Now, don't get me wrong; I was thankful for their business, but it was clear to me that I was dealing with a lot of power-thirsty, rejected people who'd paid for the ability to delegate. The graphic work was secondary; they were more interested in having someone work for them than they were with getting their seals or logos created. I've had orders where the customers wanted me to speak with them several times a day. They would not approve their designs, instead, I'd get an email that said, for example, "Tiffany, I think we're heading in the right direction, but there are a few things I want to change. Please call me so that we can discuss this." *Call? For what?* I had a revision form that they could fill out, but after having spoken with so many people like this, I came to understand that they wanted to feel powerful and important. In most of these cases, they'd want me to call them at a certain time or they'd call me whenever they were in a public place. They'd then proceed to speak to me in an authoritative tone, detailing what they wanted changed on their designs. Now, get this ... I would already have their requests in email form. I could hear people in the background and I soon realized that they were just showing off. They wanted to sound powerful and important.

The Lord kept dealing with me until I became tired of dealing with controlling, double-minded, manipulative people. After finishing a hard order, I was ready to walk away, but I opened my heart and let God speak to me.

Why close my business when I could just take the prices up like He told me to do? If I wasn't hearing from God, raising my prices would achieve the same results as closing my business. So, I did what the Lord told me to do. I took my design prices up to $149, meaning, I doubled my prices.

Things became quiet in my business for a while. I wasn't getting many orders, so I decided to revamp my site. Suddenly, the orders started pouring in. The enemy tried to convince me that if I took my prices up, I would lose the few customers I did have and he was right. I lost the bad customers and God sent me some amazing new customers who weren't controlling, nor did they have wrongful relationships with their money.

The Jezebel spirit comes to stop a business from starting and from growing. People who are bound by this spirit will oftentimes look for businesses with one or more of the three pitfalls:
1. Low prices

2. Little to no rules
3. Bad branding
4. Desperate owners

Low prices often mean that the owners don't know the value of what they are selling and therefore, they can be bullied. Jezebels are bullies and this is why low prices often attract them. There was a girl who'd reached out to me some years ago. She loved to create Facebook Timeline banners. She was very skilled at what she did, but she lacked confidence, not just in her gifting, but in herself. She looked for validation wherever she could find it. Most of all, her prices were far too low. Anyhow, she reached out to me because she was fascinated with the work I did.

One day, she reached out to me and asked me what she should do about a woman she was working with. The woman kept making her redo the banner she'd created and she kept telling her about all the famous people she knew. She told her that once the order was complete, she would introduce her to a few well-known leaders. Of course, the girl was excited initially, but after revamping that woman's flyer again and again, she came realize that the woman was more interested in controlling her than she was with getting that flyer. I told her that she was in the snare of a Jezebel spirit. I'd worked with that demon so many times that I knew its ways. I told the young woman that the woman used the names of those celebrities to get a handle on her. "She doesn't personally know them," I told her, "and if she does, her relationship with them is not benefiting her, after all, she came to you because your prices are low. If she's not benefiting from knowing them, what makes you think that she will be of any benefit to you?" The young woman agreed, but she didn't know how to break free from that woman's fangs. I ministered to her and I had to let her go and fight that demon because it wasn't my fight. My assignment was to pray for her, instruct her and hope that she'd take my advice. There was nothing else I could do. She was in the level of prophetic training that separates the prophets from the profits. As a marketplace minister, she needed to pick up her sword and slay Jezebel.

Little to No Rules: Jezebels hate rules and for this reason, they focus most of their attention on new companies and insecure people. Remember, the Jezebel spirit is a spirit of perversion, meaning, it likes to disrupt the order of things. When a business doesn't have an established system, it is easy for a Jezebel to move freely, without detection or interruption. You must establish concrete rules and stand by them. Please know that you will have to offend quite a few Jezebels on your way to the top, but this is okay, despite what others may tell you. I'm not telling you to be condescending and mean; what I am saying is you won't be able to appease everyone. Plus, if disregarding your own posted rules and prices is what you must do to satisfy a person, let that person walk away dissatisfied. I've literally refunded people who started off hard to work with, especially with extensive orders, like website orders. I have had people to start off being rude and condescending, and once I realized this was going to be the tone of our communications for the next week or so, I hit the refund button. Never be so determined to hold on to whatever money a customer has paid you that you fail to realize the true price you're paying for working with that person. It is better to work on your branding and pay for new programs and products for your company than it is to spend time earning dirty money.

Bad Branding sends a clear message to everyone who views it and that is: the owner is a cheap (or broke) person who is desperate to earn a few bucks. You end up looking like you've cut a square out of a box, wrote your company's name on it with a magic marker and now, you're standing on the side of the highway, begging folks to do business with you. In other words, you look like a beggar. When your branding is low-budget, people will not respect whatever it is that you're selling because you obviously don't respect it or, at least, in their eyes, you don't. Bad branding is worse than no branding at all. Additionally, it is a billboard for the Jezebel spirit because it speaks more about the owner's bondage than it does about the business.

Desperate Owners: Nothing attracts Jezebel more than desperation and fear. To Jezebel, desperation means you're already defeated and you're now ready to compromise. For example, let's say that a man walks into your electronics store and asks for the price of a radio you are selling. You tell him the price and he says, "Too much for me," and proceeds to walk away. At that moment, you have two choices. You can either call him back and reason with him, offering him a lower price or you can let him walk away. A desperate business owner will stop the guy and offer him a discounted rate. This sends a message to the man that the owner is more desperate than he thought. The guy would then tell the owner what he wants to pay, and then he'll proceed to tell his friends about the desperate owner. What the entrepreneur has done is unwittingly launched a "going out of business" sale. That guy's friends will walk into the business owner's store and pull the same stunt. They'll then tell their friends who'll tell their friends, and before long, the business owner will close his doors for good.

Jezebels close prophetic businesses with ease. How so?

1. **They are time-wasters who cannot be appeased —** One of the greater lessons you'll come to learn in marketplace ministry is, not everyone is looking to be appeased. Some people are just desperate to control someone. They can best be described as Jezebels without Ahabs. Try as you may, you will never please a person who has a Jezebel spirit. If that person approves some work you've done, it's only because Jezebel is about to place another order with you, and this time, he or she has more time to spare.

Jezebels close businesses by using up too much of the company's time and resources.

2. **They want more for less —** Jezebels will oftentimes find mistakes that you've made and point them out, magnify them, and try to use them to justify controlling you. For example, if you are a waitress at a restaurant, someone with a Jezebel spirit will find an imperfection on his or her spoon and point it out to you. From that moment on, Jezebel will examine everything that you do in hopes that you will give her (or him) a discount. If you don't run fast enough or jump high enough, Jezebel will ask to see your manager. A week later, she (for example) will sit in your section again just to see how much you've learned about serving her. She'll say (for example), "Remember me? I sat in your section last week and you gave me the dirty fork. Anyhow, I believe in second chances, so I'm hoping that we

have a better experience this week." From that moment on, she (for example) will expect you to serve her more than you're serving your other customers. She will even gesture or call you while you're helping another customer. If you do not come when called, Jezebel will want to see your manager again, and she'll use that experience to push for another discount.

3. **They zap you of your joy and make you hate doing what you do** — I've lost count of the number of prophetic people I know who've closed their businesses because of Jezebels. They got tired of fighting, not realizing that regardless of whether they stayed in business or not, they were still going to have to overcome Jezebels. This is just a part of the prophet's life. I have several services that I provide under my company. If I notice I'm getting a lot of orders from people bound by the Jezebel spirit, and they are ordering a

particular service, I won't stop providing that service. After all, that's what the enemy wants me to do. Instead, I'll raise my prices and tighten up on my rules. This is almost always enough to chase away Jezebel, and when it is not, the additional revision fees will chase them away.

4. **They'll go out of their way to harm your business when offended —** It's not uncommon to hear someone with the Jezebel spirit say things like, "I'm gonna report you to the Better Business Bureau," or "I'm gonna contact every news outlet I can find to report what a fraud you are!" Additionally, they will threaten to take you to court, and this isn't because you've done something wrong; the problem oftentimes occurs when you won't do business with them their way. Jezebels will go to your site, read your rules, hire you, and then, start trying to violate your posted rules. For example, let's say that you make custom

bracelets for a living. On your website, you post this rule: *Please double-check the name you submit to have added to your bracelet to ensure that it's spelled correctly. If you misspell the name, we will not assume the responsibility, but you will have to keep the bracelet and purchase another one.* A woman named Martha, who happens to be bound by the Jezebel spirit, sees this rule and doesn't like it. She has a niece named Sheila, but she's not sure how to spell Sheila's name. Instead of calling Sheila's mother, she decides to guess the spelling. She makes up her mind that the rules do not apply to her. She orders the bracelet and spells Sheila's name as Shelia. After the bracelet is finished and you send her a snapshot of it (before shipping), she sends you a message that reads, "My apologies. I spoke to my niece's mother and she said that her name is Sheila, but you have it spelled Shelia. Please correct." You go back and review the submission and just as you suspected, she's the one who submitted the wrong spelling of Shelia's name. You send her a copy of the submission and you copy and paste the rules to the email. She responds, "Common sense should have told you that it was spelled Sheila. If you're not going to correct the bracelet, give me my money back and I'll go someplace else!" Nevertheless, you have a no refund policy and she's fully aware of this, so you refuse to give her a refund. She then takes to social media to speak evil of your company. Additionally, she keeps inundating you with threatening, highly emotional emails. One day, you decide it's not worth the fight. You still have the bracelet in your office, so you decide to submit a refund to the woman and just refuse to do anymore business with her. You email her and say, "I just submitted a refund to you. Have a great day." To your surprise, she responds, "My niece's birthday passed and I didn't have a gift for her because you held on to my money. Had you refunded it when I asked you to, I would have been able to get her a gift, so I am writing you to let you know that I will be taking this matter to court." You're surprised. First, the woman didn't follow the rules, and now, she wants to punish you for enforcing the posted rules on your site. You decide not to respond. A few days later, you get an email from the Better Business Bureau and inside the email is her complaint against your company. She's also started an Internet campaign to destroy your company's credibility. She's going to sites like Yelp and Google Reviews to leave nasty, condescending reviews about your company and your character. Her lawyer advises her that she cannot take you to court because the rules are posted, so she attacks your company's name for three years. Please know that this is exactly how a Jezebel acts in business. They intentionally violate rules because they feel that they should be exempt from them. The reason a refund would not appease a Jezebel is because she (for example) does not want a refund; she wants you to violate your posted rules. She wants to bring your company under submission. The correct response, in such a case, is to stand by your rules one hundred percent. If the person starts behaving erratically, it is better to submit a refund to that person; that is, if you haven't sent the product to them or provided the service for them. After that, ignore her antics to a certain degree, but once she starts repeatedly coming after you, send her a professional email and ask that she remove all the negative reviews and stop defaming your name and your company. Don't not be moved by her emotional response. If she doesn't stop the attack, hire a lawyer to draw up a cease and desist letter and send it to her. Some people would argue, "Just give her what she wants; it would be cheaper and require less energy!" Those same people would be out of business in three years or less because Jezebel would swallow them whole. Sadly enough, as an entrepreneur, you may have to make an example out of one Jezebel to keep the other ones from following in her footsteps. Prayerfully, it will never go to that extreme, but you must be prepared for the worst if you want to receive the best.

Another thing to note is, not all Jezebels are going to approach you in a mean way. Some of them disguise themselves as prophets or just sweet old ladies (or men) looking to help. One such case happened to me back in 2013. A woman called my business line, and instead of placing an order, she started off with, "I like to tell people about me before doing business with them" (paraphrased because I don't remember her exact words).

She then went on to talk about all the noble things she'd done. I had just instituted a rule that stated that I would not sit on the phone and listen to a long discussion or sermon. My customers must get to the point so we can move forward with their orders. I hadn't posted this rule, however. It was something I'd decided in my heart. I kept trying to cut in, but she was determined to get her story out. Finally, I just sat there and listened while working on another project. She started asking me questions about myself, including where I'd gone to school. I told her that I was Holy Spirit taught; I've never attended college. She saw her opportunity right there. She said that there were many grants being given to women right now and I could apply for them. She said that she could help me get into college. I explained to her that I did not want a college degree, as silly as it may sound. God once told me that no man would get the glory from anything I do; He would get the glory and I prefer for it to stay that way. She would not let off. By this time, she'd talked for over an hour, so as you can imagine, I was a little irritated because customers who talk a lot normally don't buy much or, in most cases, they don't buy anything. I said to her that God had given me a style that's all my own. I'm not opposed to college, but it's not the direction I believe God is taking me in. After two minutes, she became forceful and condescending. Amazingly enough, she wasn't pushing the skills that college could give me; she was pushing the idea of me getting a degree. I refused. I finally told her that if she needed to order something, I could help her with that, but I wasn't going to continue discussing my personal life and plans with her. She was livid. She hung up the phone on me and thankfully, I never heard from her again.

Demonic spies often ask a lot of questions and they will tell you a lot about their personal lives. It is up to you to shut this behavior down. As I mentioned earlier, you can't get around offending some people. When I started off in business, I hated offending people so I looked for ways to avoid it. This only caused me to fall into more snares. I had to learn that offense is inevitable. Sometimes, just reminding someone of your posted rules (in a nice, professional way) is enough to offend that person, especially if he or she has no intentions of following those rules. For example, the woman who'd called me had no intentions of placing an order. She was attempting to do something you'll find that most Jezebels are skilled at doing. She was trying to create a relationship with me. She wanted a soul tie. She wanted to insert herself as a needed figure in my life; therefore she kept saying that she knew a few people and she could help me to get into college. She'd talked for more than an hour about herself before she found out that I didn't have a college degree. Once she discovered this fact, she'd found what she believed to be her opportunity to connect. Why did she want to connect? Because she'd been referred to me by someone else. She'd looked at my website and saw all the services I offered. I'm sure she looked at my personal website too (most Jezebels do). Maybe she wanted free branding. Maybe she thought I was rich. I'm not sure why she wanted to connect. What I do know is this: she wanted to connect with me and her motives were impure. She sounded friendly, but her tone kept shifting throughout the call. She kept talking about how she could help me and who she knew, but I knew without a shadow of a doubt that I was on the phone with a Jezebel (not the woman, but the spirit that was in the woman). When I got off that line, I was very frustrated with myself for allowing that situation to take place. I kept telling myself that I should have hung up on her at the five-minute mark when she would not let me cut in. I should have made it very clear that I would not stay on the phone past ten minutes. I shouldn't have discussed my plans or what God said to me with her. I was beating myself up when the Lord impressed upon my heart that I was simply learning a lesson that would help me as my business grew. I didn't waste my time; I learned to enforce the posted rules, whether online or within my heart. I also learned that when dealing with demonic spies, a marketplace minister must always enforce his or her rules. Don't let someone tell you their life's history, unless God tells you to listen. Don't let someone take up your time. Understand this, when the enemy is trying to distract you, there's something or someone he's trying to distract you from! In other words, stay alert!

Competitors

One of the instructions God gave me when I started out was this: Do not compete with anyone. Competing always puts you behind the people who offer similar products and services. It keeps them on your mind. Of course, I didn't listen at first because I was stubborn. I thought I needed to know what my competitors were doing, so I would visit a few of their sites regularly.

One day, I was trying to design a seal for a guy, but I felt empty. I couldn't think of anything, so I thought that if I visited one of my competitor's sites, I'd see something he did and get some inspiration. I didn't. Instead, I became even more confused. My energy felt zapped. I didn't know what was happening so I began to pray. Immediately, the Lord rebuked me for going to the competitor's site. He told me that my "dry spell" had everything to do with me depending on myself to come up with a design concept, rather than me depending on Him. I repented and resubmitted myself to the Lord. The ideas came, the man loved his seal and I learned a very valuable lesson. To date, I do not have competitors because I'm not competing with anyone. I focus on my assignment and not another woman or man's assignment. Do I occasionally see designs created by other designers? Yes, of course, but not always intentionally. Most of the time, I see another designer's work, it is on social media. I am drawn to seals and logos, so I will click on one when I see it to see how it looks to me. I don't use it for inspiration or ideas, even though seeing another design does stir me up sometimes.

Your competitors can and will pose a problem if you violate any rules. You see, the people who are competing with you will oftentimes feel like you've violated their market, especially if they have a degree and you don't. This is especially true if you start to dominate a market that they feel entitled to. For this reason, you must make sure that you are always operating in integrity and you aren't in violation of any laws or codes of morality. When you enter a market, people will ignore you for the first few years, but again, when you start to dominate that market, some of your competitors will look for ways to sabotage your company. They will survey your website, building or any place they see you marketing your products or services. If they find that you're doing something wrong, they will report you. This is called spying. Spies look for ways to attack.

One of the ways to grow your anointing is to trust God and to never allow the enemy to use you as a marketplace spy. There will be times when you feel tempted to check out companies who offer similar services, and this is okay if you are, for example, building your website and trying to see what all you should offer. This is also okay when you're trying to make sure that like companies aren't stealing your information, but this is not okay if you wrestle with jealousy or insecurity. You must check your motives or you will eventually allow your morality to bleed out one insecurity at a time. God had me to stay off my competitor's websites until they were no longer my competitors, meaning, I stopped trying to compete with them. With that competitive spirit lifted, my desire to visit the websites of like companies went completely away.

Some people would argue that it is good to know what your competitors are doing and this can be true to an extent, but think of it this way: If you are always checking behind your competitors, this could only mean that they are ahead of you. You must wait for them to produce something innovative and then, you come behind them to see how you can benefit from what they've produced. This line of reasoning is why so many Christian businesses have gotten left behind. To think outside the box means to first realize that there is a box and you don't want to be in it.

Basics of Business Startup

Whether you're starting an online business or a brick and mortar business, there are a few things that you need to do to ensure longevity for your company. For me, personally, my business is online because I am a service provider. I don't have a need for a building as of right now, but you may have a different story.

In addition to wisdom, you must use common sense when starting and running a business. Below are three truths most Christian business owners live by.

1. **Put God first.** I can't stress this enough. If you <u>truly</u> put God first in your business and you keep Him first, it not only will not fail, but it cannot fail. Of course, this only applies if you have a godly business; this does not apply for something that goes outside of His will, like ungodly music or yoga.

2. **Shut off all the noise.** As I mentioned earlier, when I started off in business, one of the burdens the enemy tried to put on me was the weight of other folks' opinions. Amazingly enough, these were not people who I personally knew, even though I did get some familiar resistance. A lot of the opposing opinions came from legalistic, misinformed, religious souls who thought it was their job to set me straight. Thankfully, God taught me to not be moved by what people say or do. One of tests He's told us, as believers, to perform is called the fruit test. Look at a person's fruit and ask yourself, "Do I want what's manifesting in his or her life?" If the answer is no, that person's advice is not your size. Either you're too big for it or it's too big for you.

3. **Do not hire your friends, family members or church members.** Familiarity breeds contempt. We've heard this many times, but it is true. *Of*

course, if you're married, you will work with your spouse and it's okay to hire your children if they have good work ethics. A young woman recently asked me what she should do about her friend who is now her supervisor. She said that ever since she started working under her friend's supervision, the friend has been treating her differently and this was putting a strain on their friendship. Of course, I explained to her that the issue wasn't the friend; it was her. Familiarity was in their midst and she wanted her friend to stop acting like her supervisor, even though she was her supervisor. Her complaint wasn't unique to her. Anytime you supervise someone who sees you as "on their level," you will battle with one of two issues: either that person will try to address and treat you like a co-worker, instead of a supervisor, or a power struggle will ensue.

4. **Morality over money.** There are times

of need and times of abundance, but you will never tap into abundance if you love money. The love of money leads to immorality and shady dealings. There were many times where customers of mine unintentionally overpaid me. They weren't aware of this fact until I made them aware of it. There were many cases where they thought my prices were higher than they were, and I could have taken advantage of these opportunities, but because I love and fear the Lord, I wasn't even tempted to keep their money. I explained my pricing schedule and refunded them immediately. God said if you're faithful over little, He'll make you ruler over much. I had to be faithful with the talents God gave me before He started multiplying those talents.

Starting an Online Business

Just like a brick and mortar business, there are several things you need to have and there are several things you should have.

Most businesses that permanently close their doors are closed because the owners were cheap, lazy or simply didn't have the faith they needed to succeed. As I mentioned earlier, there are some people whose companies are the equivalent of soap testers or samplers. They want to test the market before diving into it and this is not the heart of a faith-filled entrepreneur. Why not? Because if I want to test a service or a product, I won't launch an entire business to do so. I'll just test it before launching it. Additionally, some things don't fare well during testing. It takes time for people to become aware of what you have to offer. If you are impatient, you'll close your doors before you develop consistent, stable clientele or develop your own unique fingerprint on your brand, products or services. The first two or more years after startup are about you developing your clientele and maturing your brand. Understand this, when you first start off, you will be testing certain areas of the market you're in. You'll be seeing what works and what does not work. For example, if you're selling custom knit gloves, you'll want to see which fabric sells the most and which colors are a hit. You learn this through consistent sales. One of the worst things to do is assume that a particular style or color will be a best-seller and then, end up spending more money on it than you would on other styles. For example, I love elaborate designs, but I had to learn that some people like simple designs. Simple designs, to me, look incomplete, so in my infancy, I would try to help customers out by adding more to their designs than what they'd asked for. Of course, the customers would ask me to strip the designs down to only what they'd requested. I did and when I was finished, the designs looked naked to me, but the customers loved them. I had to learn that my preferences are just that: my preferences, and I shouldn't impose them on anyone else. What's average to me may look fantastic to another person and what's fantastic to me may be too busy for another person. One of the keys to success in business is to keep your opinion out of your business.

To start and run an online business, there are a few things that you must physically do as well. Thankfully, online businesses aren't as difficult to launch as physical companies because online business owners aren't bound by city codes. Below are a few tips to starting an online business.

1. **Research the market you are entering to ensure that you don't need a license or any other legal documentation.** If you do need certain documents to get started, be sure to follow the steps and pay the necessary fees to get your licensing.
2. **Write the vision and make it plain**. You need a business plan to get started. A business plan isn't just your vision for your business; it is a write-up, detailing the steps you intend to take to make that vision successful.
3. **Create a budget.** I can't lie and say

that I've created or ran my business using budgets, but I do believe that if I had, I would be more successful than I am today. However, I can say that I have invested most of what I've earned in my business back into the business or into the ministry (assignment) God has given me. Even though I once spent a lot of money on material things, I built my collection over the years. In other words, most of what I earned (even then) went back into my assignment (ministry) and my business.

4. **Sow like you're already rich.**
   Consider the widow with two mites. She gave everything she had into the offering and the Lord said she'd given more than anyone. This means that she could expect a greater harvest. Giving is a part of receiving; you can't reap a harvest if you haven't planted any seeds. Sow into the church God has planted you in and act crazy with your sowing. In other words, don't sow

out of your abundance; sow out of your lack. When we have, for example, a thousand bucks surplus, it is easy for us to sow a hundred bucks for tithes and fifty bucks for an offering. However, this means we are sowing out of our abundance and not our desperation. Desperation moves God, so if you want a fruitful harvest, ask God how much He wants you to give outside of your tithes. Don't rebuke Him when He tells you the number. Just give.

5. **Brand out of your abundance, not your lack.** We give out of our lack, but we must brand out of our abundance. What does this mean? In the beginning, you should throw every extra penny you have at professionally branding your business. One of the most damaging mistakes that some entrepreneurs make is they settle for bad branding in their attempts to save money. It is better to have no branding than it is to have bad branding. Some

people settle for poorly designed websites, unattractive brochures filled with misspelled words, and lifeless business cards. When you do this, you send a message to everyone who views your branding material that you are a struggling business and therefore cannot be trusted. This will cost you more than eighty percent of your sales, in addition to forcing you to sell your services below market value. Ask yourself this: why would I pay some local, run of the mill printer the same amount of money that I would pay Office Depot when that company's branding is sketchy? It is very important that you stay away from do-it-yourself website builders and the like in your attempt to save a few bucks. Invest the money! Sow the seeds and they'll come back over time. Some people may ask, "Well, what if I don't have the money to invest?" Time is the equivalent of money. As a matter of fact, companies pay you for your time. This means you can utilize your time by learning to <u>professionally</u> brand your business on your own. But wait — before you get started doing this, you must learn to brand before you start actually branding. This means that you can invest in a website builder and play around with it for several months or a year until you've learned to master that tool. When you can use their blank templates, and build websites that small and large businesses would be willing to pay you for, you are ready to start branding your own. Honestly, it's better to save the money and brand the right way; this will save you quite a bit of time in the long run.

6. **When choosing a domain for your website, keep it simple!** Let's say that your business is called Mary's Custom Bracelets & Broaches. It would be career suicide for you to purchase www.maryscustombraceletsandbroac hes.com, especially if you expect to get

the bulk of your sales from online customers. The best domain to consider for this would be www.marys.com if it were available or www.mcbb.com. Additionally, you could look at www.maryscustom.com, www.maryscustombandb.com, or www.marysbandb.com.

7. **If at all possible, keep your name, bio, and face off your website.** Now, if your name is Mary and you have a company called Mary's Bracelets and Broaches, it is okay to show your face, but I recommend that you avoid personalizing the business if you want people to deal with you professionally, instead of personally. Let me explain. When I started off in business, I was all too anxious for people to know the face behind their logo designs. This opened the door for a myriad of problems. One of those problems was my potential customers wanted to get to know me first and they wanted me to know them before they did business

with me. The first question potential customers would ask me was, "Is this Tiffany?" Once I acknowledged who I was, they'd tell me how proud they were of me and how blessed I was. After that, they'd start telling me about their goals, hardships and ideas. These conversations would last for more than thirty minutes, oftentimes an hour. I didn't want to be rude, so I'd sit there and listen, while my phone kept buzzing, alerting me that other callers were trying to get through. I lost a lot of money (and time) in this era of my business. The Lord eventually told me to take my face off my professional website. He explained to me that it is better for people to believe that they are dealing with a large corporation and that when they call me, they are speaking with someone who works for that large corporation. When I obeyed Him, my business flourished. Nowadays, I still get one or two people every quarter or so to research my company, looking to see who owns it, but they won't find this information on my professional site. Instead, they find themselves on my personal site, but I'm ready for them when they call and attempt to deal with me personally, instead of professionally. I no longer allow long conversations to take place. If they say, "Is this Tiffany?" I answer with, "Yes, it is. How can I help you?" I allow them to say what they want to say within a one to two-minute span. After that, I cut in and say, "Thank you for your kind words. How can I help you today?" Now, understand this, some people will get offended when you do this because they don't want to deal with you professionally (hence the reason they will conduct an extensive search to see who owns the company); they want to become personally acquainted with you. When you keep speaking professionally, to them, you are saying that you don't want their personal friendships and

this is offensive to some people.
Nevertheless, their motives are impure
and oftentimes they don't have a dime
in their accounts to pay you with. One
of the lessons I've learned after doing
business with thousands of ministers
and ministries is, people who have the
money won't talk very much. They
won't try to get personal with you
because this does not benefit them at
all. People who want to know where
you grew up, how old you are, who
you're married to, how many kids you
have, and what church you attend are
people who do not want to pay your
posted prices; that is, if they intend to
pay at all. They are time-wasters who
will ultimately cost you more money
than they bring to you, so if cutting
their conversations short offends
them, remind yourself that you can't
afford to flatter them.

8. **Research like businesses to learn
   how you can stand out from the
   rest.** Earlier in this book, I told you to

not follow your competitors and I still stick by this suggestion, however, it is good to initially look at the people who may consider themselves to be your competitors so that you can determine how to stand out. You shouldn't follow their systems or mimic their branding. Instead, look for problems that they haven't addressed and create solutions to those problems. Look for ways to simplify and improve the customer's experience and look for ways to make your company, products and services appear futuristic.

9. **Sign up for other sites using a branding handle.** For example, if your business is Mary's Custom Jewelry and Broaches, your handle should be whatever your website is. If you're using marysbandb.com, your social media handles should be @marysbandb. Additionally, you can opt to use the handle @braceletsandbroaches if you want to draw more attention to what you do,

rather than your professional name. This increases your links on Google which, in turn, gives your company a better rank with Google. For example, currently, my site is ranked number one on Google search engines, so when people google Bishop Seal Design, the first listing they see is my company. Similar companies have paid thousands of dollars to get this seat, but they have been unable to take my place. Of course, it's all God. He will give you the wisdom you need to dominate the search engines. As a matter of fact, I had a customer to call me one day and the first thing he said, "Ma'am, do you know that your company dominates the search engines? Every time I searched for bishop seals, your company's name came up." He was so impressed with how much my company dominated the search engines that he went out of his way to see who owned the company.

10. **Continuously update your site,**

adding new services, updated policies and new products. Google's spiders (robots) crawl sites daily and the sites that are updated rank higher than the ones that are rarely updated. Additionally, you want your customers to keep coming back to your site. Sites that are not updated rarely get new visitors.

11. **Advertise often.** I got deleted quite a bit on Facebook during the youth of my business because I shared my seals and logos daily. I also started tagging and messaging people to advertise my services. Even though some people consider these behaviors rude, they were effective for me. Some people found out about my company simply because they saw one of the logos through a tag. Of course, I eventually stopped doing this because I came to understand why people considered this behavior to be rude. Needless to say, I don't regret it because again, I made a lot of money through those

tags and brought a lot of attention to my business. Of course, I'm not suggesting that you tag people outside of their permission; I am merely trying to show you how effective marketing is, even when it's free. I wanted to earn one thousand dollars to use on a cruise to the Bahamas I was about to take, so one or two weeks before the cruise, I started mass marketing my services and offering discounts. I offered book cover designs for $75 and logo designs for $100. I ended up making $1,500 and I had to stop the sale because of the amount of orders I'd received. The point is, marketing works.

12. **Be faithful and let your business grow.** All businesses take time to grow. Not only do they require time, but a business's growth depends solely on how much time, money and attention the owner gives to it.

Starting a Local Business

To start and run a local business, you must

remember that your customers can see you, your employees, your building and everything in it. This means that you must ensure that you and your employees are professional in your attire and appearance, you are always wearing a smile, and your company is always clean both internally and externally. Additionally, remember that smiles are pointless if your attitude is bad. I often think about a few experiences I've had while dining out. I used to eat out every weekend by myself; I called this my date with the Lord. Because I ate out so much, I started noticing a pattern of behavior with some waitresses. I'm a tipper; I love to make someone else's day better, but I won't tip for bad service. As a matter of fact, I go out of my way to be the kindest, least disruptive customer my waiter or waitress has had, so if I say someone gave me bad service, that person gave me terrible service. Anyhow, I noticed that I would get friendly waiters and waitresses who would take my order, bring my food to me, smile and even compliment me. After that, they'd completely ignore me for the duration of my stay. There were even a few times when I'd had to stop other waitresses and ask for refills. The waiters or waitresses assigned to my table would finally reappear to bring me my ticket and they'd smile and be super friendly, hoping that their big grins would qualify them for tips. They don't. I'm always friendly, regardless of what type of service I get, but I won't sow into manipulation. Again, smiles are pointless if you have the wrong attitude or if your service is bad.

In addition to following the tips posted for online business owners, here are a few more tips that brick and mortar entrepreneurs should abide by:

1. **Be sure to check your local city and state requirements to make sure that you're up to code.** Get the proper licenses and familiarize yourself with the laws that you must abide by (city, state and federal) and lawsuits that are common in your region.
2. **Don't get the cheapest building just**

because it's cheapest. A lot of people don't realize that they often pay more for buildings that are barely up to code and located in bad neighborhoods than they would pay for decent to good buildings in better neighborhoods. How so? What you don't pay in rent, you'll end up paying in maintenance fees (higher electric bills because of the poor insulation, removing graffiti from the walls, constantly repairing or replacing broken walls and appliances, paying higher fees for theft insurance, etc.). Be sure to stop by some local businesses in decent neighborhoods and ask the owner how much he or she shells out in monthly costs. You'd be surprised to discover that the man who leases a building in a bad neighborhood, for example, pays $1,500 a month in rent, along with $2,100 in utilities each month; whereas, the guy with a building in a good neighborhood pays $2,500 a month in rent, along with

$1,100 in utility costs. The difference is in sight versus oversight. The guy in the better neighborhood looked at the overall picture, but the guy in the bad neighborhood saw the lower rent and thought he'd found a better opportunity. He hadn't. As a matter of fact, there will be some months when his monthly payments are higher than the man paying $2,500 a month simply because his utilities will fluctuate.

3. **Don't be afraid to ban or rebuke bad customers:** Remember, people bound by the Jezebel spirit often close businesses. They are narcissistic souls who want to be worshiped. They could care less that they are holding up the line. I was in Sears one day, looking for an outfit to wear to an event. I finally found something I felt satisfied with, so I went and stood in line behind a woman who was already checking out. The woman looked back at me and proceeded to take her time. She kept talking to the cashier, so much so that

she'd forgotten to take her wallet out of her purse. What should have literally lasted one minute ended up taking ten minutes. After locating her wallet, the woman took her time, counting out change, and after that, she asked the cashier to remove the staple from the receipt. She said that staples bothered her. After the cashier complied, she went on to tell her why staples bothered her. During it all, she kept turning and looking at me, to see how I was responding. I just kept smiling and looking ahead. Finally, she started talking with the cashier about the traffic and then, she turned to address me about the traffic. I smiled and agreed with her, reminding myself that I was building my character. Before she left, she took her time to put her receipt in her wallet, place that wallet neatly in her purse and slowly grab her bag. I could tell that she didn't want to leave, so I walked alongside her and handed my items to the cashier. The woman then walked away and the cashier thanked me for my patience. Now, because this happened in Sears, there was nothing the cashier could do. But for a smaller company, that one customer could put a company out of business. How so? People who have the Jezebel spirit often become repeat customers at any establishment that tolerates their narcissistic ways. In a way, they unofficially become broken pillars of those companies. They will repeatedly go into brick and mortar businesses, usurp the authority of the business owner and proceed to dominate every customer service agent's time. They will be rude to other customers, and if their behavior is not dealt with, they will permanently close the doors of any business that tolerates them.

4. **You need rules!** Let's say that you're running a restaurant and a few of your male customers like to come into your company shirtless and barefoot. This

attire or lack thereof is establishing a belief in the minds of every other customer regarding what class your restaurant is in. If you tolerate their behavior, you will lose a lot of your classier customers and before long, your restaurant will be crawling with half-dressed souls, hopping around and complaining that they've stepped on something sharp. Rules allow you to establish the environment and reputation you want and they keep you from losing control of your business's image. They also protect you from frivolous lawsuits.

5. **Have your cameras ready and a lawyer on standby:** Slip and falls are the most common lawsuits that brick and mortar companies deal with. Having grown up in impoverished areas, I know that there are a lot of people who take advantage of any opportunity they can find to steal a few bucks. For example, if you mop in the middle of the day, you will be

targeted. The best time to mop is when the store or building is closed. All too often, anxious employees start mopping while customers are in the store and this only opens the door for immoral opportunistic souls who earn the bulk of their income through lawsuits. Therefore, you need to have clear, working cameras in place, as well a good lawyer.

6. **Always make repeated trips to the bank to ensure you're never holding a lot of money at any given time.** Many store robberies are the result of employees or former employees telling their immoral friends about a company's inner-workings. It is unwise to protect yourself from outside attacks, while being lazy, tolerable and unproductive on the inside. Your most dangerous threats are oftentimes the people you train. For this reason, you want them to see you making repeated drops at the bank during daylight hours. You

should also have someone with you, like a spouse, police officer or someone who a thief does not want to encounter.

7. **Hire security or provide free services or products for officers:** One wise move some companies have taken is hiring security guards, but the ones who could not afford them, started providing free services and snacks for police officers. This resulted in their companies becoming places that police officers frequented, thus, thwarting many possible robberies from taking place. For example, having a seating area, free coffee and doughnuts is oftentimes enough to become an officer's hot spot. There was a very popular nightclub in Mississippi that was causing many other nightclubs to go out of business. People from surrounding cities and states traveled just to get into that club. There was no end in sight; the club was prospering until one day, it

suddenly closed. Eventually, people found out how the club came to such an abrupt end. Police officers used to park at the club to monitor the crowd and control the traffic. Fearing that the heavy police presence would scare away some of his customers, the owner did a news interview and complained about the police presence. After that, the Chief of Police stopped the officers from going anywhere near that club. As a result, a lot of fights broke out, a lot of codes were violated and less than a month after the interview, the club closed its doors for good. The point is, having officers frequent your business is a blessing, unless you're doing something criminal.

8. **Have a solid return policy:** Do not let people bring things back simply because they have changed their minds. You need to have a solid return policy in place. For example, clothing stores are well aware of the fact that

some people buy their clothes, wear them to an event, and then, bring them back. To control this behavior, they won't accept anything that looks or smell worn.

9. **Find out the best temperature to set your thermostat to:** Companies that are too hot in the summer and too cold in the winter usually get their best sells during the fall months. Not long after fall is over, they go out of business, plus, it is a city code violation in most cities to allow a building to reach certain temperatures.

10. **Hire mystery shoppers to test your employees:** Many employees have run their employers out of business because of their poor attitudes and shady dealings. Therefore, it is good to hire mystery shoppers every few months to test the people who work for you. Your goal is to find people who are thankful for the jobs they have, so much so that they treat your company

like it's their company. Just like you shouldn't settle for bad branding, you should never settle for bad customer service.

Whether you are running an online business or a brick and mortar company, again, you must remember to put and keep God first. As a marketplace minister, it is important that ministry be your first objective. I'm not telling you to attempt to evangelize your customers; I am saying that God should be seen and felt in your company, on your website and more importantly, in your character. Success is not having a lot of money; success is being able to properly manage the portion God has given you. Every level of success has a bottom and a top. You must ascend through each level, and every time you fall because of procrastination, pride, fear, intimidation, or sin, the goal is for you to repent, learn from your mistakes and get back up again.

Tidbits to Grow By

Marketplace ministry is not for the faint at heart. The reason for this is, there is a lot of wisdom to be had in this arena. It is important for us all to understand that wherever there is wisdom, there will be warfare. The greater the depth of wisdom that's available, the greater the warfare will be to get to that wisdom. For this reason, there are enemies of the marketplace that every believer should be aware of. Oftentimes, these enemies identify themselves as Christians. They speak our language, join our churches and sing our songs. They memorize scriptures, adapt to our systems and will even attempt to evangelize the lost. Nevertheless, they are not submitted to God. They are religious, legalistic people who've come to contend with the faith. They promote ungodly mindsets and attempt to establish impossible moral codes for believers to be bound by.

They write and preach right-sounding messages designed to break the church, demonize Christian leadership and exalt themselves as heroes of the faith. Their messages sound people-centered, but they are truly self-centered. For example, one such enemy is the legalistic soul who believes that no Christian should profit from their businesses, especially if what they're selling could be deemed as ministry related. People like this genuinely believe that a Christian artist should write songs, pay for the studio time to record those songs, pay to have the songs mastered, pay the graphic designer to design the cases for their new albums, and when it's all said and done, they should give those CDs away freely. Why? Because they're Christian and they should be broke, hungry and destitute — at least, that's what the enemy has convinced them of. These same people will often quote Matthew 19:24 without following it up with Matthew 19:26. They would have argued with Apostle Paul and said that the tents he made should be given away freely because some people have nowhere to stay. Remember, Judas complained about the woman pouring perfumed oil on Jesus' feet. He said that the bottle should have been sold and the money should have been given to the poor, but the truth was, Judas was a thief who walked with the disciples of Christ. This made him look like a disciple but, in truth, Judas was a self-centered, money-loving hypocrite. Such people will buy a secular artist's entire album, even when the lyrics are raunchy. They will throw money at strippers and repeatedly pay the people at the drive through window to hand them a bag of death. Now, this doesn't mean that those who think this way are an enemy of God (only He determines this); it does mean that they lack knowledge, and if they're not careful, they will align themselves with the world and become a part of its system. The moment a scandal breaks out between the world and the church, they will be the first ones to condemn the church and use their knowledge of church culture to gain leverage against it.

James 4:4 (ESV): You adulterous people! Do you not know that friendship with the world is enmity with God? Therefore, whoever wishes to be a friend of the world makes himself an enemy of God.

When I first started creating seals and logos, I received a few messages from people, telling me that I was outside the will of God. One woman even attempted to give me a dark prophecy. As silly as this sounds, she did this because she didn't understand Facebook. She logged into Facebook and saw my logos on her home page because obviously she was on my friend's list. She didn't realize that there was a difference between her home page and her personal page, so she assumed that I'd posted my designs to her timeline (I didn't know how to tag people then, so her assumption was due to her lack of understanding regarding Facebook). For this reason, she posted a very ungodly and condescending message to my page. Reeling with anger, she posted what she tried to pass off as a damning message from the Lord. I knew it wasn't from God because she'd written things about me that were not true. Her message read this way (I don't remember the exact words): "Stop posting those logos to my page! I did not give you permission to write on my page! Because you have done this thing, hear the Word of the Lord." From there, she started passing her emotional outburst off as a prophecy. She was one of the many people I had to pass by to deliver what God placed in me. As a marketplace minister, I could not let her get to me. I deleted her comment (and her) and I refused to dignify the enemy (Satan) with a response. I prayed for her and moved on.

Understand this: where there is no opposition, there is no position. Opposition is the opposing of your position. In marketplace ministry, you will meet many people who will oppose you for no obvious reason. One of the most common will be empty vessels who are fueled by jealousy. Another will be vessels who are full of potential, but are too afraid to push their way through the shallow waters (ungodly relationships, offense, church hurt, abandonment). These people are truly sons and daughters of God, but the problem is fear has placed an anchor on them. One thing you'll come to know about stuck people is, they hate to see other people moving.

Another enemy of the marketplace minister is the minister himself or herself. Two important questions to ask yourself (and be completely honest with your answer) are: Am I intimidated by my own anointing? Am I intimidated by the vision God has given me? If you're honest with yourself, the answer is likely yes. The average believer fears his or her own anointing. This is largely because we are creatures of habit; we tend to create comfort zones for ourselves that we try to stay near. Therefore, God allows the storms of life to come our way. The storms come to drive us out of our shallow comfort zones and into the perfect will of God. In other cases, storms come to make us anchor ourselves in the Word when we are moving too fast.

We are also afraid of our own potential because of what we've come to believe about ourselves. Maybe your parents told you that you'd be a great basketball player and the whole world would gather someday to see you play. Now, your Father in Heaven is telling you that you'll be a great man (or woman) of God someday and the whole world will tune in while you pray. We are afraid of our potential because of how far we've come in our attempts to pursue the identities we've accepted for ourselves.

Until you walk in your prophetic anointing, you have not yet found yourself and, for this reason, you will travel aimlessly through life, looking for clues as to who you are. After you get tired of looking, you will pick up the identity that the people around you celebrate the most, or you'll learn to identify yourself the way your family identifies you. When God comes along and hands you a compass, you will realize that you've been heading in the wrong direction most, if not all, of your life. It is only natural for you to panic because the truth is, acknowledging that you are heading in the wrong direction means turning around (repenting), starting over (getting a new heart and a new mind) and heading in the opposite direction (serving).

What am I Gifted to Do?

There are many business ventures that a marketplace minister can get into, but the most profitable (spiritually and monetarily) is the arena that God has graced you to operate in. For example, if you are graced to do landscaping, it will not benefit you much to enter the field of medicine. Sure, doctors make a lot of money (if we are measuring their pay by the standard pay in America), however, had you entered the field of landscaping, God may have blessed you to earn ten times more in a week than the average doctor earns in a year. However, if you get caught up measuring greatness using the world's standard of measurement, you'll rob yourself of your potential. Additionally, you could end up making more money as a doctor, but hating every minute of what you do. This isn't success; it's the paid edition of slavery.

Like most people, I didn't know what I'd grow up to do professionally. At one point in my life, I'd planned to become a psychologist. I didn't want to deal one on one with people like a psychiatrist does, I wanted to study the human mind. I didn't realize that this was the minister in me attempting to find ways to help people outside of God (I wasn't saved back then). Despite my desires to study people, I loved creating things. I got into my mother's fabric and made skirts for myself. I also loved decorating, making gift baskets and playing around with makeup. I was creative; that was and is my niche. I wasn't just creative in one arena; creative people are creative period. Additionally, I loved writing music and books (on notebook paper). The point is, who I am bled through who I'd learned to be and the same is true for you. You just have to ask the Lord to open your eyes to see the obvious.

Multi-gifted and Confused

One of the most common questions people ask is, "What if I'm multi-talented? Which gift should I start marketing first? The answer is simple. Take a page from Jesus' life and learn to market God, storing up treasures for yourself in Heaven, and then, start marketing your business. Of course, when I say, "market God," I'm not saying to profit from ministry; I'm saying to focus more on evangelism and restoration so that you can learn how to approach people. This is seeking first the Kingdom of God and all His righteousness. After that, He (God) will add everything else (ideas, strategies, witty inventions) to you.

Next, always focus first on the gift that God gives you the most understanding and provision for. There were gifts that I was aware of and I attempted to market them prematurely, only for me to invest into them and reap a lesson behind them. I learned that just because I can do something doesn't mean that it's the right time for me to do it. Pray about every gift you have and master the one that God brings to your attention the most. Keep the other ones fresh through study, practice and prayer.

A Time and a Place

There's a time and a place for everything. Of course, this is common sense; then again, in some situations, you need to use wisdom to discern what to say and do versus what not to say and do. For example, I'm an entrepreneur, author and blogger. What I do professionally is what I do daily, meaning, I'm absorbed in this world. This also means that when I speak, I often speak about business, books, and so on.

I'm invited to teach at different venues and when I go, I must remind myself that an innocent conversation on my part could be misinterpreted as me trying to promote myself, my services or my books. For this reason, wisdom has taught me when to remain silent and let someone else take the lead in the conversation versus me taking the lead. As a marketplace prophet, you must be careful regarding what you say, who you say it to and where you say it at. This means that even though sometimes you'll have a lot to say, you must refrain from speaking. This is especially true when you're at someone else's venue. In addition to this, never see the church as a place to promote yourself, your brand or your books. Sure, some churches have bookstores, but you must follow the church's protocol to get your book into their stores. When you go to the sanctuary, you must enter it with thanksgiving and praise. You should never enter it with motives.

John 2:13-17 (ESV): And He found in the temple those who were selling oxen and sheep and doves, and the money changers seated at their tables. And He made a scourge of cords, and drove them all out of the temple, with the sheep and the oxen; and He poured out the coins of the money changers and overturned their tables; and to those who were selling the doves He said, "Take these things away; stop making My Father's house a place of business."

Godly Connections are Needed

Please note that a godly connection is brought together by God, and not your ambition. Also, you can connect with a godly person and still have an ungodly connection. This is especially true if your motives or the other person's motives are impure.

In marketplace ministry, there are several seasons that you will likely go through. One of those seasons is the season of being alone. Now, this may not be true for everyone, but it is true for many marketplace prophets. This is because, in our dark seasons, we picked up friends and habits that were ungodly. In our seasons of religiousness, we picked up friends who were double-minded and sketchy. When we were babes in Christ, we befriended (and dated) folks who were representatives of the sin that we were still being delivered from. For this reason, we must be sanctified (set apart) and purged. This doesn't mean that we'll be completely alone; it does mean that if your only friends and associates are people who love the sin they're in, you'll more than likely be delivered from all of them. In other words, you could spend a few seasons alone. Another believer may have a few God-fearing friends that God will allow them to remain connected to.

Once God determines that we are ready for the people He wants to connect us with, He will introduce us to them one need at a time and one level at a time. Godly connections are often brought together by need, but not by neediness. This means that I may have something that another believer needs or vice versa. Wisdom will tell us if those connections are seasonal or permanent. One of the biggest setbacks to marketplace ministers is when we unintentionally mislabel relationships. Think about the contents of a can. How disappointed would you be if you bought some cans and told one of your children to fill up each can with beef, chicken and fish, only to have that child mislabel the cans? You load up your truck with the cans that are labeled "chicken" and head over to the market to sell your meat. A few hours later, a few disgruntled customers come and start berating you because they went home to eat their chicken, only to find out that the cans were filled with fish. You'd be angry because that simple mistake could cost you a lot of customers and ultimately cost you your business. Additionally, once those cans were opened, you could not repackage that meat. It had to be thrown away, which means that you've lost quite a bit of inventory. This is what happens when we mislabel relationships. We expect a person to be one thing (friend, confidant) when they are another (someone posing as a friend for the sake of getting free mentoring).

Godly connections are purpose-driven and time sensitive. This means that we, as marketplace ministers, need to stay submitted to God so that we will be in place and on time when called. We need to be sensitive to His Holy Spirit; that way, we won't spend a whole lot of time learning lessons that we could have avoided.

Common Snares

In my time as an entrepreneur, I've met quite a bit of people and one of the snares I've watched people repeatedly fall into is what I call the multi-level marketing snare. First, let me say this: I am not against people joining multi-level marketing companies, but I am against folks getting stuck in these companies because they produce systems of defeat. I worked in multi-level marketing several times when I was desperate to make money and one of the greatest lessons I learned during that season was, even though these programs can work, multi-level marketing is better suited for people who have money to throw away during the learning process. They are not for people who are struggling financially and often live paycheck to paycheck. This is because you must invest quite a bit of money into a market that may not be effective in your city or community. Large companies understand the inner-workings of target marketing, but they won't tell you, for example, that those expensive knives won't sell well with men, people who make under $25,000 a year and in lower middle-class communities. For example, I remember working for a company selling expensive knives and other cutlery. I would go to the meetings and get pumped up, but after leaving, I had to face one turn down behind the other. One of the guys who was doing well with his sales was an upper class, handsome young man who honestly didn't need any extra money. I think he just wanted to sharpen his marketing skills, which is great. He sold a lot of knives effortlessly, not because he marketed better than me or the other people who had joined the program, but because he was a member at a local country club and had access to wealthier people than we had. Other success stories that I heard while involved in multi-level marketing companies came from professionals who'd used some of the money they made in their careers to buy their products. Greater inventory equals greater profit. I didn't have any money to buy thousands of dollars' worth of products, so my return wasn't all that great. One fact that you must consider is this: When purchasing products from a wholesaler, your price is determined by how much you buy. For example, Walmart can go to a wholesaler and buy 100,000 boxes of toilet paper for ten dollars a box (this isn't the actual figure; it's just an example). Another small store who cannot afford 100,000 boxes of tissue may end up buying 1,000 boxes of tissue for twenty-five dollars a box. Because they bought less, they had to pay more. Because they paid more, they must sell their products for more. So, that twelve pack of toilet paper that you could buy from Walmart for $7.99 would cost $14.99 at a smaller store. This is because both companies are for-profit businesses, and amazingly enough, even though their prices are different, Walmart often makes more money in profits for each individual sale than small business owners make.

Multi-level marketing is a great tool to learn the ins and outs of business ownership, but again, I would not suggest making it your official business. Many of the people I know who've gotten caught up in this system have heavily marketed products and services for years, and then, a couple of years later, they were involved with an entirely different multi-level marketing company. Of course, I would tell them to get traditional jobs and use the money they earned to fund their own businesses, but because they'd gotten caught up in the systems (government) of multi-level marketing, they kept investing in another man's dreams.

Another snare comes from people who swear they can make your company and your name great if you'd only give them favor (or discounts) with your company. In the infancy of my company, I came across a lot of people, for example, who would use a manipulative tool that has come to be known as name-dropping. Name dropping is when a little-known or unknown person uses the name of someone who is well-known (oftentimes a celebrity) to gain favor with others. Truthfully, they would hold me on the phone for hours at a time, telling me stories about themselves and their dealings with well-known people. They would often refer to those people by their first names; for example, someone would say in reference to T.D. Jakes, "Like I told Thomas — man, you can't be dropping that level of revelation without giving me a warning first. But he's a cool guy — very humble. Anyhow, I'm gonna make sure I tell him about your company because his entire ministry team needs seals. As a matter of fact, I have a meeting with him on Tuesday." What you'll notice most about people like this is, they want discounts, even though they claim to be well connected or wealthy. Additionally, they do not want to follow your posted rules. Lastly, if you feed into their lies or over-exaggerations, they will keep coming back to you to experience feeling important. This means that they will take up a lot of your time. Nowadays, I am not impressed with big names or titles; my focus is on completing the transaction, so I don't get these types of people a lot, but when I do, our exchanges are often comical.

The last snare I want to mention is the person who talks entirely too much and wants to know about you personally. People like this have no money. All they have are their many words and they will waste your time talking about themselves, their charitable acts and asking a bunch of pointless questions about your life. As I mentioned earlier, you will offend some people; it's inevitable. You don't do this intentionally, but you won't be able to avoid it. Again, I cannot stress this point enough: people like this do not have any money to pay you with. The end of their long, drawn out conversations will often sound like this, "Well, man (or woman) of God, it was very nice talking with you. I truly thank God for you and as soon as I get my money together, I'm definitely gonna be working with you. Tell me again, how much money do I need to save?" Honestly, they want you to be so impressed or saddened by the things they've shared with you that you respond, "No charge. How can I charge you after everything you've shared with me?" I know that I'm not gonna say this, so I cut these conversations short.

Now, don't get me wrong. I do have some actual customers who I've spoken for hours with, but this was oftentimes after the transactions were completed or I'd worked with them in the past and knew they were people of integrity. Because I work with leaders, I've received a lot of wisdom, revelation and prophecies, but the key to winning was knowing who to speak to and when to speak versus who to limit my conversations with and when to enforce those limitations. When someone keeps trying to flatter you, that person has no money. When a person challenges your rules or policies, that person does not understand honor, and therefore, lacks integrity. When a person has integrity, that person will focus more on paying you than flattering or challenging you. That person will complete the transaction regardless of what your price is and then, he or she may ask a few questions.

Common Mistakes

Just like there are common snares designed to ensnare the marketplace prophet, there are common mistakes that many entrepreneurs make. Below are 12 of those mistakes.

1. **Prematurely launching a company:** We often do this when we get overly excited and that excitement causes us to become overly anxious.

2. **Taking too long to launch a company:** When God gives us ideas, He wants us to start researching and investing in those ideas. We are to launch them when He tells us to launch them, but all too often, believers procrastinate because of fear. As a result, they watch helplessly as other people supernaturally receive what was once their ideas and those people invest the money and the time needed into launching those ideas. How horrible of a feeling it is to watch someone else prosper from an idea that God once entrusted you with.

3. **Compromising:** A lot of Christian business owners fall for what I call the devil's settlement offer. In civil court, a defendant can offer the person suing him a settlement offer. This happens when the defendant realizes that the party suing him has a solid case against him. To ward off the bad press attention and save money, the defendant will offer to settle the matter, oftentimes offering the suing party less than what he or she is asking for. Satan does the same thing. When he realizes that he will not be victorious, he will offer to settle with you. For example, in exchange for you not venturing out and expanding your business overseas, he may offer you a local building, backed by the support of your city. This may look like a great offer when you don't have the funds to expand your company and you are struggling financially, but understand this: if Satan is offering to settle with you, it's only because you've already

won and he knows this.

4. **Spending too much time on fruitless ventures:** Again, whatever you sow the majority of your time into will be what you reap the most from. If you sow more time into your traditional job, you will reap more from your paycheck than you do from your business. This sounds good, but your employers have already established, through your hourly or salaried wages, how much you are worth to them. This means that there is a cap on your pay. With your business, however, there is no cap. I understand that not everyone can invest forty hours into their businesses each week, but I also understand that the size of your reward will always match the size of your investment. If you're making minimum wage, the last thing you want to do is keep reaping a minimum harvest when you can step out on faith and eventually pull down a greater harvest.

5. **Telling your ideas to others before you birth them:** When we get excited, we often become too open. For this reason, I implemented a new system in my life to counteract the emotional system I'd bound myself to. So, whenever I'm overly excited, I intentionally avoid phone calls and of course, I won't call anyone. I pray a lot and ask the Lord for help with keeping my mouth shut. In the past when I would tell my plans to people prematurely, I would end up dealing with a lot of unnecessary warfare. Some ideas can be released, but most should be kept until they are cleared by God to be released.

6. **Trying to bring people with you who God has not approved:** Because many of us have dealt with a lot of bad people in our lives, it goes without saying that every time we encounter decent people, we want them to grow and prosper with us. Nevertheless, we soon find that there are many doors

that won't open for us until we understand that decent isn't good enough. In other words, better doesn't mean good; it simply means that we're experiencing an improvement in the quality of friends we have because we have matured. However, as we continue to grow, we will notice that the faces in our lives will continue to change until we finally grow up in God and are able to have and maintain friendships with God-fearing people who love God as hard as we do.

7. **Being too cheap:** I've said this, but I must reiterate — you cannot be a cheapskate when it comes to your business. Think of it this way. Pretend that you are a single woman who's just started dating an educated and successful young man. He takes you to the cheapest restaurants and asks you to not venture outside of the one-dollar menu. When he takes you to the beach, he parks a mile away from the beach so he won't have to pay the

parking fees. When you invite him to church with you, he puts a five-dollar bill in the offering tray and asks the usher to bring him back three one-dollar bills in change. You try to give him the benefit of the doubt, thinking that maybe he's saving money to buy a new house, but every time you see him, he's spending money on himself. Your last date with him was at the mall; he took you to the food court and told you not to spend over five bucks. After that, you walked with him through several stores and watched him spend hundreds of dollars on name brand clothes for himself. Would you continue dating this guy? Most women wouldn't because he's made it painfully clear to them that he is self-centered, cheap and inconsiderate. This is how many entrepreneurs treat their businesses. Consequentially, their businesses reciprocate by giving them a laughable return.

8. **Letting people take too much of**

your time: Time is the equivalent of money. Even more, time is greater than money because we get to determine how much we charge people for our time. So, one woman may charge you ten dollars an hour because that's all she feels her services are worth, but another woman may charge $250 an hour for her time. When we don't know the value of our time, we'll charge too little for it and we'll also let people freely take it away from us. I've entertained many fruitless conversations as a business owner, and I had to learn to stop doing this.

9. **Making an idol out of your business:** Never take a creation and place it above the Creator. It's easy to make an idol out of your business because of the level of time and money you must invest into your business. Nevertheless, you must remain prayerful and take time off if God says that you need a break.

10. **Taking too much time off:** Always

remember that we are creatures of habit. We create and operate in systems; therefore, we tend to fall back into the systems that we are most adapted to. So, when you're tempted to take long breaks from working, please understand you're not really taking off. An old system that has not been broken is simply reclaiming your time. You are having a love affair with your business, but you are married to an old system. Ever since I've been in business (six or seven years now), I have never taken time off, except for times when I've traveled. This is because I knew that I was developing a new system in my life and I had to follow it through to establish it. Once the new system became my default, I had to keep running it to ensure that I didn't get rusty or return to the system of procrastination.

11. **Overcharging:** Honestly, I believe that greed is the number one assassin of Christian businesses. Oftentimes,

people overcharge because they don't want to endure the process of growing wealthy; they want to get rich quick. As a result of this mindset, they become the anchors that keep their businesses from going forth. I've seen people overcharge for everything from jewelry to e-books. When I started creating seals and logos, I decided to develop a system that would allow me to charge more than fifty percent less than what other seal and logo creators charged. This system would allow me to spend far less time designing the graphics, which meant that I could make more money per hour versus what most designers make per design. I remember considering this concept: I could actually be the J.C. Penney of seal and logo designs, selling high-quality, expensive designs to my customers, or I could be the Walmart of seal and logo design. As the Walmart, I would produce high-quality, inexpensive designs for less, but I'd sell more designs in the process. To do this effectively, I'd have to develop a time-saving system. I chose to go the Walmart route. Use this same system when, for example, starting your own perfume line. You'd need to decide whether you want to brand your fragrance as a high-end fragrance sold in stores like Macy's or brand it as a common fragrance sold in stores like Target and Walmart. Both markets are great; the high-end market has more risks and may take longer to generate income, but it could ultimately produce the greatest return if you invest in it properly. The common market has less risks, far less startup fees, and has the potential to generate a great return with far less effort.

12. **Not establishing rules, guidelines, and limitations:** Rules and guidelines represent walls; they are what protect your business from thieves and immoral people. My posted rules have saved me from many heartaches and

potential Jezebel encounters. Every time I had a problem with a customer, I created a new rule to protect me from having that problem with any other customers. I didn't waste a bad experience by complaining about it. I took the opportunity to learn more and to use those experiences to fortify my company.

As a marketplace prophet, always remember that God is the CEO and Founder of your business. As such, He will determine when you're promoted and what promotion you receive. He won't advance you just because you believe you deserve to be promoted; God looks at our hearts and decides how much promotion we can handle. How much promotion can you receive before you become prideful? How much promotion can you handle before you start believing that you don't need God? With every new level, we must battle higher ranking demons than the ones we once battled, but honestly, the battles don't get harder. This is because our faith grew every time we defeated a level. Nevertheless, if the last level almost killed us, God will oftentimes work with us to build up our faith; this way, we don't end up being overwhelmed when we encounter more opposition. Remember, opposition is the opposing of your position, so every time God is ready to promote you to a new position, you can expect some opposition. Additionally, after you've gotten past the demonic forces and people who have hindered you, the greatest opposition that you will have to face is yourself. If you overcome your reflection, you will have reached a level of success that most men could only dream of.

Minding God's Business

Jesus was a carpenter, which means that He specialized in carving wood. Remember, wood is symbolic of humanity, so Jesus' natural profession was connected to His destiny. The Bible refers to us as vessels, meaning, we are like wooden ships. We carry God's merchandise (our experiences, wisdom, knowledge, and understanding) from one person to the next. When we proclaim Christ as our Lord and Savior, we are saying that the merchandise on our ships is godly. However, just like natural ships, our cargo has to be inspected and just like natural ships, we are destructible. There are five dangers that we must look out for and they are:

Stowaways: Again, a stowaway can be a person who is trying to ride the wave of your anointing. That person is trying to access the blessings of God without dying to herself or himself. This is very similar to when the people of the earth decided that they wanted to illegally access Heaven by building the Tower of Babel. Stowaways try to build relationships with people for the purpose of elevating themselves.

Illegal Merchandise: In the natural world, people have been known to board ships and attempt to smuggle drug paraphernalia and other illegal items into countries. Our illegal merchandise can be what the Bible refers to as the doctrines of demons, lack of forgiveness, ungodly associations, and anything that God tells us to rid ourselves of.

Shipworms: Also known as the termites of the sea, shipworms bore into wooden hulls, thus, causing severe damage to ships. For us, however, our shipworms are the small foxes (sins, belief systems) that destroy the vine (see Song of Solomon 2:15). These are the little issues that go unnoticed until we begin to sink.

Drunk Captains: It is not unusual to find an intoxicated captain attempting to navigate the seas on a ship or boat. Likewise, the Bible tells us to be sober-minded. Of course, this isn't just a reference to avoiding alcohol or being responsible with your alcohol consumption, it is also referencing having the mind of Christ. Paul asked the Galatians, "O foolish Galatians! Who has bewitched you? It was before your eyes that Jesus Christ was publicly portrayed as crucified" (Galatians 3:1/ ESV). The Greek word for "bewitched" is baskainó, and it means to fascinate or overpower. The Apostle Paul was simply saying that the Galatians were not in their God-given states of mind. An intoxicated believer can be someone who's fascinated or bewitched by false doctrines, under the control of another human being, or someone who's dabbling with the occult.

Pirates: Pirates are thieves who navigate the seas looking for opportunities to kill, steal, and destroy. Most pirates of the high seas illegally board and hijack the ships they want to plunder, kill the people on board, steal all of the valuables that they can find, and once they're done, they sink the ship. Of course, the pirates who come after believers are demonic spirits looking for opportunities to kill us, steal everything God has imparted in us, and destroy our legacies.

As vessels, we can sink into sin, depression, self-condemnation, and the like. This is why God said in Isaiah 59:19 (ESV), "When the enemy shall come in like a flood, the Spirit of the LORD shall lift up a standard against him." The enemy is always trying to drown or overwhelm us. This is especially true for marketplace prophets because we have the keys to God-approved wealth. Satan doesn't want us to be wealthy because that puts too much power in our hands. For this reason, he twists scriptures in his attempt to confuse believers. For this reason, some people say that money is the root of all evil when, in truth, the Bible says that the LOVE of money is the root of all evil (see 1 Timothy 6:10). Ecclesiastes 10:19 (ESV) reads, "Bread is made for laughter, and wine gladdens life, and money answers everything." Because money answers everything, the enemy is determined to silence it by ensuring that believers don't get their hands on it. One of the tricks of the enemy is to convince believers that to desire wealth is to be in sin, when this is not true. To desire to consume wealth upon yourself is error (see James 4:3), but it is selfish to not desire to be wealthy. How so? People who want just enough to provide for their own families aren't considering the widows, orphans, homeless people, and individuals who need God-fearing saints to help them with their situations. This means that they have no desire to open homeless shelters, feed the poor, clothe the naked, or so on. This is selfish behavior. Additionally, Satan has people working for him who identify themselves as Christians, and these people condemn, criticize, persecute, and attempt to destroy any believer who is wealthy. They hate to see leaders prospering and this mentality is not the heart of God. It is the evidence of their ignorance or the demonic doctrine to which they are bound. The enemy uses them to throw accusations (darts) at true believers.

Revelation 12:10 (ESV): And I heard a loud voice in heaven, saying, "Now the salvation and the power and the kingdom of our God and the authority of his Christ have come, for the accuser of our brothers has been thrown down, who accuses them day and night before our God."

John 10:10 (ESV): The thief comes only to steal and kill and destroy. I came that they may have life and have it abundantly.

As vessels, we navigate from one kingdom (mindset) to the next. Every mindset is what we've set our minds to believe. In other words, if we believe God, we set our hearts and minds to His Word. This means that we are in His Kingdom and His Kingdom is in us. This also means that we'll sail from glory to glory. If we do not believe God, we have unwittingly agreed with the enemy. This means that we have set our hearts and our minds to whatever belief system the enemy has exposed us to.

Noah's job wasn't to navigate the ark. He simply had to build it, fill it, and board it. From there, God would do the rest. This is very similar to what we must do as believers. We are the vessels, so we're already built; our job is to be filled with the Holy Spirit, stay on board (in agreement) with Him, and let Him take us into the perfect will of God. As entrepreneurs, we must treat our companies like our bodies. We are temples of the Holy Spirit, and therefore, we must allow our companies to become places of habitation for the Holy Spirit. When we do this, like Noah, we slowly begin to exercise our God-given dominion in the realm of the earth. In other words, we start expanding God's Kingdom. We defeat worldly systems by establishing godly businesses that are run by godly systems. To mind God's business means to continue Jesus' assignment here in the realm of the earth. We continue to expand the gospel by taking back every system that the enemy has hijacked. We demolish strongholds (ungodly mindsets and demonic opposition) and set the captives (unsaved, demonically-bound, brokenhearted) free, and we do this by entering and dominating the marketplace. Will we experience resistance?

Yes! Absolutely. Where there is no opposition, there is no position. Will we experience dry seasons? Maybe. Every vessel has to dock from time to time so that it can be unloaded and reloaded. One thing is for sure, we will never sail empty. But the question we must always ask ourselves is this: What am I full of? If you don't know the answer to this question, simply look at where you're heading. You wouldn't be taking demonic doctrines, strife, fornication, or any other sin to godly places, but you will be taking the Word of God to ungodly places. This means that if you're filled with the Word and driven by love, you are in the will of God and God is behind your wheel. He's the Captain of your ship; He is your anchor.

To mind God's business means to put and keep God on the throne of your heart, not attempting to share that throne with anything or anyone else. It means to move when God says move and to stay put when God tells you to stay put. It means to trust God with your business, even when His instructions make no sense to your natural mind. It means to cast away and cast out anything and everything that causes you to sink. Consider what a ship's crew does when a boat is sinking. They cast off what is referred to as jetsam. Dictionary.com defines "jetsam" as: *goods cast overboard deliberately, as to lighten a vessel or improve its stability in an emergency, which sink where jettisoned or are washed ashore.* In our case, we have to cast down imaginations that exalt themselves against the knowledge of God, and cast out some of the mindsets that we value when those mindsets are causing us to sink. We also have to cast out the enemy every time he manages to board our hearts.

To mind God's business means to put God first in your business. It means to forsake self and others for the sake of spreading the gospel and destroying the works of the enemy. This means that we are not just marketplace prophets; we are prophets in the marketplace, taking back everything that the enemy stole from God's people. Myles

Monroe once said, "The wealthiest places in the world are not gold mines, oil fields, diamond mines or banks. The wealthiest place is the cemetery. There lies companies that were never started, masterpieces that were never painted. In the cemetery, there is buried the greatest treasure of untapped potential. There is a treasure within you that must come out. Don't go to the grave with your treasure still within you" (Reference: Myles Monroe). In other words, don't leave this earth until you are completely empty. Don't waste one experience (trip) or one word complaining about your experiences. Get up and be who God has designed you to be, keeping in mind that we are created in His image. What does this mean? He is the Creator; we are His creations, therefore, we are creative. In layman's terms, don't waste an opportunity to reflect God's image through your words and your works. The marketplace is yours for the taking. Now, go forth and take it.

Lightning Source UK Ltd.
Milton Keynes UK
UKHW02f1907160118
316277UK00006B/605/P